NELSON'S FLAGSHIP AT COPENHAGEN

HMS ELEPHANT

The men, the ship, the battle

THE NELSON SOCIETY©

ISBN No. 0-9537200-2-0

Written and Compiled

By

Eric Tushingham and Clifford Mansfield

THE NELSON SOCIETY

NELSON'S FLAGSHIP AT COPENHAGEN

HMS ELEPHANT

The men, the ship, the battle

Contents

LIST OF COLOUR ILLUSTRATIONS

FOREWORD

HMS Elephant was built at Bursledon on the River Hamble of "timber and plank of the growth of England". I was very pleased to discover recently that there is an Elephant Boatyard within half a mile of where she was built and that a bicentenary party was held there in 1986 to commemorate her launch.

We are most grateful to Eric Tushingham and Clifford Mansfield of The Nelson Society for producing this companion volume to "HMS VANGUARD at the NILE - the men the ship, the battle" and "The Men who fought with NELSON in HMS VICTORY at TRAFALGAR". The amount of work and time it must have taken has to be read to be believed. Members of Family History Societies now have a further opportunity to search for their naval and military forbears in the muster lists.

Nelson chose to shift his flag from the *St. George(98)* to the two decker *Elephant(74)* commanded by Captain Foley. She was the same design as the *Vanguard,* having a shallower draft, more suited to the waters of Copenhagen Sound, bringing echoes perhaps of their experience at Aboukir Bay. Nelson was not in overall command at Copenhagen and suffered great frustration at the lack of resolution displayed by Admiral Sir Hyde Parker. Here we have an eye witness account from Colonel William Stewart, who commanded the Rifle Corps, of the famous incident when Nelson saw Signal No 39 in the midst of the battle. Henry Newbolt must have read this too, as he quotes Nelson verbatim, in his famous poem- "Admirals All":-

Splinters were flying above, below when Nelson sailed the Sound.
"Mark you I wouldn't be elsewhere now" said he "for a thousand pound ".
The Admiral's signal bade him fly, but he wickedly wagged his head.
He clapped his glass to his sightless eye and "I'm damned if I see it" he said.

Perhaps it is not surprising that Colonel Stewart called his eldest son 'Horatio'. Here is also the story told by a Doctor at the Naval Hospital at Yarmouth when Nelson visiting one of his sailors who had also lost his arm said "Well Jack, you and I are both forever spoilt for fishermen".

He spent the next three years trying to get Copenhagen medals for his men, but discovered in 1804 that the Government was against them, for fear of upsetting the Danes. It was 1847 before Queen Victoria put this right. Perhaps it was better late than never for some.

With this book it is possible to get the feel of the battle, how it was fought and who fought it. I, for one, am very grateful for this insight and it will surely give great pleasure to all naval historians both to professionals and amateurs like myself.

Anna Tribe

Raglan Monmouthshire
March 2001

Anna Tribe
Vice President, The Nelson Society

INTRODUCTION

The Nelson Decade (1995-2005) embraces the bi-centenaries of the four major sea battles, St. Vincent, the Nile, Copenhagen and finally Trafalgar in which Admiral Nelson was either engaged or commanded. These battles and other major events in the personal life of the Admiral have been and will be marked by Conferences, publications, visits and this publication is a contribution of The Nelson Society to the commemoration of the battle of Copenhagen, 2 April 1801.

Commemoration, not celebration, is the dominant theme in remembering these great events of the past and the courage and sacrifice demonstrated by those on both sides fighting for their countries is fully acknowledged.

"The Men who fought with NELSON in HMS VICTORY at TRAFALGAR" by Charles Addis MBE, containing the muster list of the ship and biographies was published by The Society in 1988 and this was followed in 1998 by "HMS VANGUARD at the NILE – the men, the ship, the battle".

The present publication continues the series containing not only the muster list of Nelson's Flagship, HMS Elephant, but also the names of the foot soldiers who were to be employed in storming the batteries although their services were not required. Strangely a Danish blockship was named "Elephanten" and in her position was the receiving point for the flag of truce and later developments.

The amount of time and patient research required in producing the book was considerable and our thanks extend to Eric Tushingham, and to Clifford Mansfield who contributed much and, in particular, the military dimension.

Dudley Pope's book on the Battle was titled "The Great Gamble" and the irony of it all was that, had the communications been better and the news of the assassination of the Tsar on the 24th March been available, maybe the battle would not have been fought but then it has to be seen in the context of the struggle against Napoleon.

Ironically, the name of Nelson is often associated in the continental mind with the expedition led by Lord Gambier in 1807, part of the continuing european conflict, which led to the abduction of the Danish fleet and destruction of the city, the bankruptcy of the country and the loss of Norway. Such were the consequences of war.

Research is a continuing process and the Editor would be delighted to receive any information on the men named in the muster list.

The Nelson Society is most grateful to those who have contributed to the production of this work and it will be a most be a useful addition to any Nelson Library.

March 2001

Derek Hayes
Executive Chairman
The Nelson Society

PRELUDE

Following the battle of the Nile (1 Aug., 1798) Napoleon Bonaparte was temporarily confined in Egypt and the powers of Great Britain, Austria, and Russia acted in unison to seek to restrain the territorial ambitions of France. This cohesion was short lived and, as Napoleon returned to defeat Austria – Czar Paul of Russia, encouraged by Napoleon, withdrew from the coalition and Great Britain found herself alone. The reverse worsened when, on 16 December 1800, an Armed Neutrality was formed between Sweden, Denmark, Russia and Prussia. With her successful navy Britain had been used to arbitrarily imposing her will at sea against all neutrals and their trade. Materials, which might be used by the navy, such as timber and rope, were of particular concern. The Armed Neutrality posed the likelihood of action involving the navies of former allies who indicated they would provide armed escorts for their merchant vessels.

Napoleon Bonaparte had by this time been elected First Consul through a new constitution which gave him sole control in France and their conquered neighbours, enabling him to establish himself and his family as the new ruling dynasty.

Earlier on 10th November 1800 Nelson had received a gold sword from the City of London in appreciation of his actions at the Nile (1 Aug 1798), and on the 20th of the month took his seat in the House of Lords. The King delivered a speech to Parliament, in the light of the activity in the Baltic.

'The detention of property of my subjects in the ports of Russia, contrary to the most solemn treaties, and the imprisonment of British sailors in that country, have excited in me sentiments in which you and all my subjects will I am sure, participate. I have already taken steps as this occasion indispensably required; and it will afford me great satisfaction if they prove effectual but [he warned] if it shall become necessary to maintain against any combination the honour and independence of the British Empire, and those maritime interests on which both our prosperity and our security must always essentially depend, I enter no doubt either on the success of those means which, in such an event, I shall be enabled to exert, or the determination of my Parliament and my people to afford me a support proportioned to the importance of the interests which we have to maintain.'

On 1st January 1801 in a general promotion of Admirals, Lord Nelson was made a Vice-Admiral of the Blue, joining his old commander The Earl of St. Vincent, who was in command of the Channel Fleet. He hoisted his Flag in the St. Josef, at Plymouth on the 17th., having Captain Hardy as his Captain. The 'Naval Chronicle' reported that when Lord Nelson's Flag was hoisted, it was 'cheered by the whole Fleet'.

In correspondence to his friend Earl Spencer.K.G., Nelson wrote:-

TO THE RIGHT HONOURABLE EARL SPENCER, K.G.
Plymouth Dock, 17th January 1801

My Dear Lord,

I was with Lord St. Vincent yesterday, when Sir Hyde Parker's letter arrived, announcing his appointment to the North Sea command. This naturally led to a confidential communication as to my views and present situation, and he gave me leave to tell you our conversation. Next to getting a command which I was candidate for, whenever Lord Keith gave up his, of course my pleasure would have been to serve under him, but that circumstance had so altered since my arrival, that it was almost certain I should go to the Baltic'; and I relate our communication on this subject. The Earl was very handsome to me, and hoped that, by a temporary absence of a few months, I should not lose my San Josef, the finest Ship in the world; and only one voice points out the Formidable as the Ship fittest for me, for real and active service. I told him the King's desire about Captain Grindall, to which he desired me to say, as his opinion, that Captain G. Could suffer no inconvenience in keeping the San Josef in order, till my return, or some new arrangement takes place. He mentioned several other Ships, degrees below the Formidable, but entreated I would not go in the Windsor Castle; that she was such a leewardly Ship, that he knew she would break my heart; for that I should often be forced to anchor on a lee shore, and never could lead a Division in a narrow Sea, like the Baltic. Having related this conversation, I shall leave the subject, as far as relates to myself. It naturally enlarged on the best means of destroying the Danes, &c., and I found him clearly of opinion that 10,000 troops ought to be embarked, to get the Danish Arsenal. I told him this matter had been canvassed with your Lordship, but the difficulty was, where to find such a General as was fit for the service, to which he, of course, was forced to acquiesce but General Simcoe seemed the only man.

Having stated this conversation, I have only to add, what you, my dear Lord, are fully satisfied of, that the service of my King and Country is the object nearest my heart and that a First-Rate, or Sloop of War, is a matter of perfect indifference to your most faithful and obliged.

NELSON

The letter carries, even at this distance, the energy and enthusiasm of the man and his seamanship. For readers familiar with his history the clear affection for the *San Josef* is not a surprise, nor the restlessness for activity and involvement. On 17 February 1801 the Admiralty ordered Nelson to place himself under the orders of Admiral Sir Hyde Parker, Kt. He was directed to take a fleet of eighteen ships of the line and a variety of frigates, bombs and fireships assembled specifically for duty in the Baltic, in support of diplomatic approaches. Routine administration was not neglected in the preparation for the expedition:-

TO THE PRINCIPAL OFFICERS AND COMMISSIONERS OF HIS MAJESTY'S NAVY

St. George, Torbay, 20th February, 1801

Gentlemen

Having hoisted my Flag on board the St. George, and finding her not fitted for a Flag, I request you will be pleased to give the necessary directions for her being fitted as such on her arrival at Portsmouth, as she is now under weigh for that anchorage. The boats are not calculated for the service I am to be employed on. I have further to request they may be altered as I direct. I am,, &c.,

NELSON AND BRONTE.

In a further letter to Earl St. Vincent on 1st March Nelson wrote:-

'....Time, my dear Lord, is our best Ally, and I hope we shall not give her up, as all our Allies have given us up. Our friend here is a little nervous about dark nights and fields of ice, but we must brace up; these are not times for nervous systems. I want Peace, which is only to be had through, I trust, our still invincible Navy. I have not seen Captain Thesiger here, I shall receive him with much pleasure; if he is still in Town pray send word to him to meet me.........'

Lieutenant-Colonel the Honourable William Stewart of the Rifle Battalion was appointed to command the Troops on the expedition and his account of the events proved fascinating. His notes on the preparations included the following:-

' On the 27th February, in the forenoon, the troops proceeded to South Sea Common, awaiting orders to embark. Lord Nelson arrived from London about ten am. He sent for me immediately on his arrival, to Major-General Whitelock's: on first acquaintance with Lord Nelson, I witnessed the activity of his character; he said that 'not a moment was to be lost in embarking the troops, for he intended to sail next tide. Orders were sent for all boats, and the whole were on board of the men-of-war, before midday. Lord Nelson, in three hours after, left the Sally-port for the St. George; this Ship was commanded by his old friend Captain Hardy, and was under considerable repair at Spithead. No time, however, was to be lost; the caulkers and painters were detained on board, and we proceeded with them to St. Helen's, Lord Nelson observing that 'if the wind proved fair in the morning, they should be sent up the harbour, but if unfair, no time would have been lost.' The wind became fair in the course of the night, and we got under weigh at daylight on the 28th; I do not remember by what number of Ships we were accompanied. Nothing particular occurred until our arrival in the Downs: the seine was frequently hauled, by Lord Nelson's directions, and the eagerness and vivacity which he showed upon the occasion, to the great delight of the seamen, early pointed out to me the natural liveliness of his character, even in trivial matters.'

Colonel Stewart also noted that His Lordship was rather apt to interfere in the working of the Ship, and not always with the best success or judgement – at which stage he would leave it to the Officer of the Watch. As these developments were taking place, much to Nelson's frustration, his Commander-in-chief moved with deliberation rather than energy and an opportunity for an early strike was lost.

On 2nd March 1801, Lord Nelson sailed in the *St. George* from Portsmouth, with seven sail of the line, frigates, and small vessels, for the Downs, and shortly after, arrived at Yarmouth, the rendezvous of Admiral Sir Hyde Parker's Squadron. Nelson was disappointed to find his Commander-in-Chief ashore but rising early as usual he placed himself, with Colonel Stewart, outside Sir Hyde's door at eight o'clock but signally failed to generate any haste in the preparations. Sir Hyde contented himself with routine administrative matters as he sought to gather his fleet together for the expedition. Colonel Stewart was to note that Nelson's desire would have been to sail with the available ships to impose himself in the vicinity of Copenhagen and add the threat of force to negotiations with the Danish government. Possibly as a result of correspondence from Nelson Sir Hyde Parker received a letter from the First Lord to the effect:- "I have heard by a side wind that you have an intention of continuing at Yarmouth till Friday, on account of some trifling circumstances. I really know not what they are, nor did I give myself the trouble of inquiring into them, supposing it impossible, after what you have written in your letter to Mr. Nepean (Secretary to the Admiralty), that there could be the smallest foundation for this report. I have, however, upon a consideration of the effect of your continuance at Yarmouth an hour after the wind would admit of your sailing would produce, sent down a messenger purposely to convey to you my opinion, as a private friend, that any delay in your sailing would do you irreparable injury. The force you have with you is certainly equal to the first object, and there are many, very many, questions that must be determined entirely by the prompt and vigorous execution of your orders. You will, I am sure, on considering this subject fairly, think that I could not give you a stronger proof of my friendship than by conveying this opinion to you in the way I have done".

The squadron sailed from Yarmouth on the 12th March, and consisted of : -

London 98	Sir Hyde Parker Knt. Admiral of the Blue
	First Captain Domett; Second Captain Robert Waller Otway
St. George 98	Lord Nelson, K.B., Vice Admiral of the Blue
	Captain Thomas Masterman Hardy
Bellona 74	Captain Sir Thomas Boulden Thompson
Defence 74	Captain Lord Henry Paulet
Ganges 74	Captain Thomas Frances Fremantle
Monarch 74	Captain James Robert Mosse
Ramilies 74	Captain James William Taylor Dixon
Russell 74	Captain William Cuming
Saturn 74	Captain Robert Lambert
Warrior 74	Captain Charles Tyler
Ardent 64	Captain Thomas Bertie
Agamemnon 64	Captain Robert Devereux Fancour
Polyphemus 64	Captain John Lawford
Raisonable 64	Captain John Dilkes
Veteran 64	Captain Archibald Collingwood Dickson
Glatton 54	Captain William Bligh
Isis 50	Captain James Walker

Frigates:	*Desiree 40, Amazon 38, Blanche 36, Alcmene, Jamaica 26, Hyaena 20, Arrow 20, Dart 30, Pylades 18 Cruiser, Harpy*
Bomb-vessels:	*Terror 8, Volcano 8, Explosion 8, Heela 8, Zebra 8, Sulphur 8, Discovery* 8,
Fire Ships:	*Otter and Zephyr*
Gun-brigs:	*Biter 12, Hasty 12, Blazer 12, Bruiser 12, Tigress 12, Force 12, Pelter 12, Teazer 12, Sparkler 12*
Cutters:	*Fox 12, Hazard 6* Schooner: *Eling 14* Luggers: *Rover 14, Lark 14,*

The squadron was joined later by:-

Defiance 74	Captain Richard Retalick (and later Thomas Graves, Esq., Rear Admiral of the White)
Zealous 74	Captain Samuel Hood Linzee
Edgar 74	Captain George Murray
Elephant 74	Captain Thomas Foley
Vengeance 74	Captain George Duff
Brunswick 74	Captain GH Stephens

Invincible 74 was also directed to join the Fleet but was sadly lost with four hundred men off Happisburgh in unfortunate circumstances. After refitting at Chatham for service in the Baltic she sailed on the 14th March 1801. After calling at Yarmouth to collect her orders, left by Admiral Sir Hyde Parker, the pilot ran her onto a shoal, after cutting away from the main channel. The tragedy might have been avoided and time saved had Sir Hyde sent his orders down to the Thames where the vessel was being prepared.

TO ALEXANDER DAVISON, ESQ.

Latitude 57° No., 16th March 1801

Our weather is very cold, we have received much snow and sharp frost. I have not yet seen my Commander-in-Chief, and have had no official communication whatever. All I have gathered of our first plans, I disapprove most exceedingly; honour may arise from them, good cannot. I hear we are likely to anchor outside Cronenburg Castle, instead Copenhagen, which would give weight to our negotiation: a Danish Minister would think twice before he would put his name to war with England, when the next moment he would probably see his Master's Fleet in flames, and his Capital in ruins; but ' out of sight out of mind,' is an old saying. The Dane should see our Flag waving every moment he lifted up his head. I am, &c.,

NELSON AND BRONTE

Nelson suffered more frustration as his commander-in-chief stopped hourly to test the water depth as they approached the Skagerrak, turning away from land on the approach. Admiral Sir Hyde Parker had been chosen to command the fleet on the basis of his knowledge of the Baltic but his journey to Copenhagen proved to be a fitful meander – hardly the purposeful imposition of the threat of force to stiffen negotiations. It is instructive to make a crude comparison of the two men:-

> Parker was 62 years of age the son of Admiral Sir Hyde Parker and had spent much of his early career under the wing and sponsorship of his father. Four years on station in the West Indies had produced considerable personal wealth due the energies of his captains in the seizure of contraband.
>
> Nelson was 43 years of age, the son of a rector, initially sponsored by his uncle Captain Suckling, but thereafter he had progressed through energy and skill at some physical cost, losing the use of one eye and one arm in a series of engagements distinguished by his fearlessness and leadership.

At the time Nelson's personal life was in turmoil as he had travelled overland from Italy to Yarmouth in the autumn of 1800 with Sir William and Lady Hamilton who carried Nelson's child. Arriving in London they established a household together and Nelson severed links with his wife in a quite brutal fashion. After a questionable period in Italy Nelson welcomed a return to sea as second in command and applied himself to the task with gusto and enthusiasm.

From the Kattegat, Sir Hyde Parker wrote, with a note of the vessels under his control, to the Chargé d'affaires, Mr. Drummond, seeking the view of the Danes on the ultimatum from the British government. At the time Nelson finally managed to speak to his commander-in-chief and subsequently wrote to Troubridge, one of the 'Band of Brothers' from the Nile:-

'It being moderate I got on board the London yesterday for an hour, for whatever inattentions may be shown to me, nothing of respect shall be wanting on mine. I was glad to find that he was determined to pass Cronenburg and to go off Copenhagen in order to give weight to our negotiator, and I believe this conduct will give us peace with Denmark. Sir Hyde told me, on my anxiety for going forward with all expedition, that we were going to go no further without fresh orders. I hope this is all right, but I am sorry, as I wish to get to Revel before the departure of the Fleet. We should recollect it is only twenty hours' sail from Cronstadt, and the day the ice is open they sail…..I suppose we shall anchor this evening about 8 o'clock, between the Koll and Cronenburg, not only to prepare for battle, for no signal is yet made, although I believe several have followed my example. I have not had a bulkhead in the ship since last Saturday. It is not so much their being in the way, as to prepare people's minds that we are going at it, and that they should have no other thought but how they may best annoy their enemies.'

The reference to 'bulkheads' in his letter is indicative of Nelson's desire for action – the bulkheads being removed as a prelude to action, allowing free movement across the decks to manage the guns. By contrast Admiral Sir Hyde Parker chose to anchor a hundred miles from Copenhagen to await a response from Mr. Drummond – a choice which unfortunately put the fleet at risk due the onset of storms, snow and ice. The conventions of the day required that diplomatic exchanges were couched in French and perhaps deliberately the British note was in English prompting a curt rebuttal to Drummond together with his passport. After gathering British residents the *Blanche* with Drummond, and the rejected British note, returned to the fleet which was now anchored off the island of Sælland. Nelson was summoned to the *London* at the same time as Nicholas Vansittart, special envoy to Copenhagen. Views were expressed as to the preparedness of the Danes and assessment of the defences noted:-

Cronenburg Castle, Elsinore – garrisoned and some 200 cannon;
Floating batteries, gunboats and hulks in the approach channel to Copenhagen;
Island forts of Trekroner and Lynetton;
Ships-of-the-line in various stages of preparation;
And additionally the Middle Ground shoals which were a significant hazard, confining a seaward approach to a channel running roughly NNW and parallel to the coast.

Nelson suggested two options for an assault. Approaching from the North by the Sound some ships would probably be crippled and lost and a favourable wind for the assault would not allow crippled vessels to be recovered. Hearing that the strength of the defences was at the head of the line, Nelson suggested the attack could be made at the tail. The fleet going through the Sound to the South and sailing North through the Kings Deep.

Denmark is at the entrance of the Baltic, her capital, Copenhagen, on the shores of the Sound, the usual passage between the North Sea and the Baltic, and exposed to attack from the sea (Figure 22???). The city was vulnerable to bombardment from the sea. A narrow channel separated the city itself from the naval dockyard which was on a slender island. Offshore was the Middle Ground shoal between which ran a channel known as 'The Kings Deep'. Access to the harbour, dockyard and city was usually from the north and the entrance was guarded by shore batteries. At the actual entrance was the unfinished Trekroner Battery – a fort being built on piles in shallow water.

Additionally it was reported Sweden was sending fighting vessels and that the Russians were seeking to free their ships from the ice. Frustrated by the hesitancy of his commander-in-chief Nelson had noted:-

'The difficulty was to get our Commander-in-Chief either to go past Cronenburg or through the Belt, because, what Sir Hyde thought best, and what I believe was settled before I came on board the *London* was to stay in the Cattegat, and there wait the time when the whole naval force of the Baltic might choose to come out and fight – a measure, in my opinion, disgraceful to our Country.

I wanted to get at the enemy as soon as possible and strike a home stroke, and Paul was the enemy most vulnerable, and of the greatest consequence for us to humble.'

The discussion persuaded Admiral Sir Hyde Parker that a passive role risked the possibility, as the ice melted, of Russian intervention before the Danes could be brought to action. It was finally agreed the fleet would pass Cronenburg, enter the Sound, and pass the Middle Ground Shoal to a position to the south of Copenhagen and the Danish defence line. On 29th March Nelson wrote:-

'Received directions from Sir Hyde Parker to take under my directions ten sail of the line, four frigates, four sloops, seven bombs, two fireships and twelve gun brigs which have to be employed on a particular service…'

As Nelson assembled his squadron for the assault the balance of the fleet remained under the control of the Commander-in-Chief:-

London 98	Sir Hyde Parker Knt. Admiral of the Blue First Captain Domett; Second Captain Robert Waller Otway		
Zealous 74	Captain Richard Retalick	*Defence 74*	Captain Lord Henry Paulet
Ramilies 74	Captain James William Taylor Dixon	*Saturn* 74	Captain Robert Lambert
Warrior 74	Captain Charles Tyler	*Vengeance* 74	Captain George Duff
Brunswick 74	Captain GH Stephens	*Raisonable* 64	Captain John Dilkes
Veteran 64	Captain Archibald Collingwood Dickson		

THE BATTLE

Admiral Sir Hyde Parker finally having given Nelson full discretion to conduct the assault, offered an additional two sail-of-the-line to the ten which Nelson had requested. During the discussion some diffidence had been expressed as to the threat from the Navies of Sweden and Russia; again to the frustration of Nelson who declared:- 'The more....the better....I wish they were twice as many, the easier victory, depend on it.' Nelson transferred his flag to the two decker *Elephant* on 26th March as it had a shallower draught than the three decker *St. George* . He no doubt felt at home as it was of the same design as the *Vanguard*, his flagship at the Nile. For three days contrary winds becalmed the Fleet but on the 30th they weighed and sailed without opposition through the Sound. Having anchored about midday the Commander-in-Chief, accompanied by Nelson, and some of the captains designated for the attack, took a schooner to reconnoitre the harbour and channels. It was noted that the Danes had removed navigation buoys from the channels, had commenced strengthening their defences including the Trekroner battery, and gathered a flotilla of defence vessels.

Thence a bout of preparations occupied Nelson as he prepared his squadron for the engagement, involving detailed instructions including the manufacture of buoys to mark the Middle Ground and Holland Deep. On the night of the 30th March Nelson took the *Amazon*, with the remarkable Captain Riou, to further examine the Northern Channel and the defence line from the east. The position and composition of the defence line was noted, together with the shore batteries. Shots were fired at the *Amazon* during the survey. On the night of the 31st March Nelson was again engaged in a small boat seeking to determine the course of the channels and the approach to Copenhagen. On the morning of the 1st April the fleet moved to anchor off the NW of the Middle Ground. When the time came for the signal to Nelson's squadron to weigh it was said the cheer could be heard throughout the fleet. The *Amazon* with Captain Riou acted as leader and pathfinder to the squadron which was favoured by a following wind as it negotiated the Holland Deep to the east of the hazardous Middle Ground, finally anchoring in Kings Deep, about two miles from and to the south of the enemy. The Danes had earlier seen the British fleet approach from the North and might reasonably expect an assault from that direction. Nelson, with his eye for the advantage of surprise, did the unexpected, choosing to approach the battle from the south, and was favoured by the perverse wind which took him south for his preparation, then turned the following day to take him north into the fight! As the defenders hastily reinforced their vessels and shore batteries Captain Hardy, being rowed by muffled oars, sounded warily around the leading enemy ships – so close they heard the sentries conversations.

Finally Nelson sat down to dinner with his fellow captains and was seen to be in the highest spirits as they toasted a leading wind and success! As the captains returned to their vessels Nelson, Riou and Foley prepared the written orders for the battle. During the course of these preparations, Captain Hardy returned about 11pm to report the depth of water up to the defence line of ships. The orders were completed about 1am and passed to six clerks whose task was to transcribe them for the vessels of the squadron. It was reported that Nelson ignored pleas from his servant Tom Allen that he should rest but continued throughout the night to chase the progress of the clerks who finally finished their labours about 6am. By then Nelson was up having breakfasted, and he signalled for his captains at 7am and by 8am had delivered his battle orders. Captain Murray in the *Edgar* was to lead and the land forces were advised they should be ready to storm the Crown Battery as soon as it had been silenced.
At the Nile only four signals were made by Nelson as commander to his squadron.
At Trafalgar an outline plan had been agreed and minimal signals were made before the battle was joined.
Uniquely at Copenhagen his General Orders were specific; painstakingly drafted, and, copied by his clerks for the instruction of his captains. They commenced:-

> 'The arrangement for the attack is as follows but as Vice-Admiral Lord Nelson cannot with precision mark the situation of the different descriptions of the Enemy's Floating Batteries and smaller vessels lying between their two-decked ships and Hulks, the Ships which are to be opposed to the

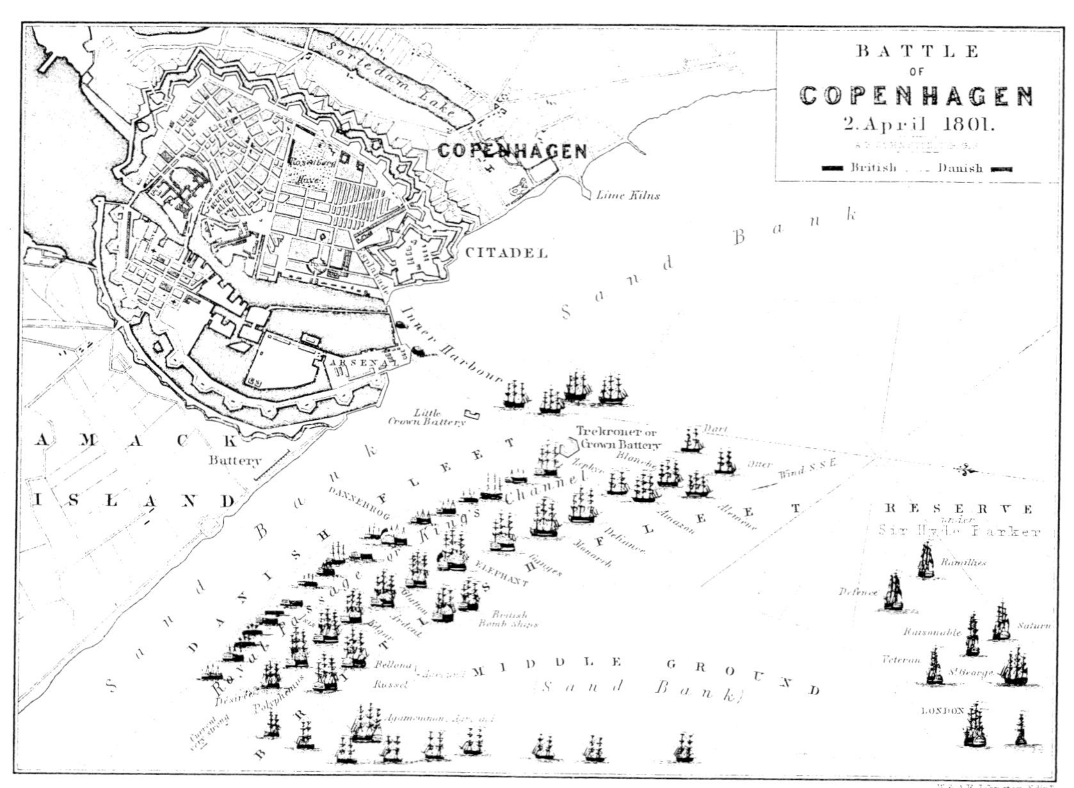
BATTLE
OF
COPENHAGEN
2. April 1801.
British
Danish
COPENHAGEN
Sortedam Lake
CITADEL
Lime Kilns
Sand Bank
Inner Harbour
Little Crown Battery
Trekroner or Crown Battery
AMACK ISLAND
Battery
DANISH FLEET
DANNEBROG
King's Channel
Royal Passage or King's Channel
BRITISH FLEET
ELEPHANT
British Bomb Ships
MIDDLE GROUND
Sand Bank
RESERVE
under
Sir Hyde Parker
Wind S.S.E.
Dart
Otter
Zephyr
Blanche
Amazon
Alcmene
Defiance
Monarch
Ganges
Glatton
Ardent
Isis
Edgar
Bellona
Russel
Désirée
Polyphemus
Agamemnon
Current very strong
Ramillies
Defence
Raisonnable
Saturn
Veteran
St George
LONDON
WILLIAM BLACKWOOD & SONS, EDINBURGH & LONDON.
W. & A.K. Johnston, Edinr

Floating Batteries will find their stations by observing the stations of the Ships to be opposed to the two-decked Ships and Hulks.'

Edgar, Ardent, Glatton, Isis, Agamemnon, ***Elephant****, Ganges, Monarch, Defiance, Russell, Polyphemus*

The sequential detail thereafter marked the vessels composing the defence line by name and/or (by way of identification) the supposed number of guns carried. Ships of the line were given secondary targets on the assumption of success in subduing the enemy vessels. The order encompassed the role for flat bottomed boats (for boarding), launches (carrying anchors and cables), and fireships directed under the orders of Captain Riou. The aim was to overwhelm the southern defences before progression northwards and towards the capital. Each vessel carried a pilot, generally from the merchant vessels though some were from the Navy. As preparations were finalised they were invited on board the *Elephant* between 8-9 o'clock but showed some hesitancy about negotiating the channel and avoiding the Middle Ground. The Master from the *Bellona* volunteered to lead which prompted the rest and at this they returned to their vessels and the squadron weighed for their appointed battle order. The *Edgar* was the first into position, anchored in 7 fathoms, but suffered some damage before gaining her place. The *Polyphemus*, and *Isis* followed but *Bellona* and *Russell* grounded prematurely on a shoal though still within range of enemy targets. The *Agamemnon*, Nelson's favourite also grounded on the Middle Ground. On the *Elephant*, Nelson saw what had occurred and, ignoring the advice of his pilots as to the whereabouts of the shoals, altered his course successfully, and, with a flutter of signals, the remaining ships followed. They were led until they gained their positions abreast of the enemy vessels. (Figure 21) With a favourable following wind the vessels anchored by the stern and were broadside to their opponents. It was noted that the action commenced at five past ten, with the first half of the squadron engaged in half an hour, and a general battle being joined by half past eleven. The *Elephant* was in the centre as planned opposite the *Dannebrog* (62) with the Commander of the Danish Fleet, Commodore Fischer. Ahead, each by half a cable, were the *Ganges, Monarch* and *Defiance* – and behind Captain Bligh in the *Glatton* which caused considerable damage to the *Dannebrog* with its massive carronades. Captain Riou in the *Amazon* took his frigates *Blanche, Alcemene* and *Dart* into an unequal contest with the Crown Battery guarding the entrance channel to Copenhagen.

Accounts of the progress of the battle range from individual anecdotes on either side through to the account reported by Nelson to his Commander-in-Chief. In this brief publication we have reprinted a contemporary account by the Commanding Officer of the Copenhagen Naval Base (Page ??), which gives a Danish perspective and provides insight into the circumstances which influenced the dogged, brave and determined resistance to the assault. One anecdote was from Mr. Ferguson, Surgeon to the Rifle Corp, who said:-

> ' At the Battle of Copenhagen I was amongst the companions of the hero. The attempt was arduous in the extreme, no common mind would have dared to conceive it; but it was united to the exalted enterprise of Lord Nelson. As his was the invigorating spirit of the Council that planned the attack, so in the execution he only could have commanded success. During the interval that preceded the Battle, I could only silently admire when I saw the first man in all the world spend the hours of the day and night in Boats, amidst floating ice, and in the severest weather; and wonder when the light showed me a path marked by buoys, which had been trackless the preceding evening. On the 1st April, in the afternoon, we took our departure with twelve Sail of the Line, and a proportional number of smaller Vessels, from the main body of the Fleet, then lying about four miles below Copenhagen, and coasted along the outer edge of the shoal called the Middle Ground, until we doubled its furthest extremity , when the Fleet cast anchor. This shoal, of the same extent of the seafront of the Town, lies exactly before it, at about three-quarters of a mile in distance; the interval between it and the shore had deep water, and is called the King's Channel; there the Danes had arranged their Line of Defence as near the Town as possible. It consisted of nineteen ships and Floating Batteries, flanked at the Town's extremity by two artificial Islands at the mouth of the Harbour, called Crown Batteries, and extended for about a mile along the whole front of the Town, leaving intervals for the batteries on shore to play.

As our own anchor dropped at eight in the evening, Nelson emphatically called out, 'I will fight them the moment I have a fair wind'. He spent the whole night in consultation. About half-past nine AM of the 2nd April the signals of the different Ships having been made, repeated, and answered, we had the mortification to see the *Agamemnon* get upon the edge of the shoal, on the first attempt to leave her anchorage, *Russell* and *Polyphemus;* and in addition to all this, the *Jamaica* frigate, with a convoy of gun-boats and small craft, having fallen in the counter-current, made the signal of inability to proceed. A mind less invincible than Nelson's might have been discouraged; though the Battle had not commenced, yet he had approached the Enemy; and he felt that he could not retreat to wait for reinforcements, without compromising the glory of his Country. The signal to bear down was still kept flying. His agitation during these moments was extreme; I shall never forget the impression it made on me. It was not, however, the agitation of indecision, but of ardent, animated patriotism panting for glory, which had appeared within his reach, and was vanishing from his grasp.'

Colonel Stewarts narrative of the events included:-

'The action began at five minutes past ten. In about half an hour afterwards, the first half of our Fleet was engaged, and before half past eleven, the Battle became general. The *Elephant's* station was in the centre, opposite to the Danish Commodore, who commanded the *Dannebroge*, 62, Commodore Fischer, Captain F. Braun. Our distance was nearly a cable's length, and this was the average distance at which the Action was fought; its being so great, caused the long duration of it. Lord Nelson was most anxious to get nearer; but the same error which had led the two Ships on the shoal, induced our Master and Pilots to dread shoaling their water on the larboard shore; they, therefore, when the lead was a quarter less five, refused to approach, nearer, and insisted on the anchor being let go. We afterwards found, that had we but approached the Enemy's line, we should have deepened our water up to their very side, and closed with them: as it was, the *Elephant* engaged in little more than four fathom. The *Glatton* had her station immediately astern of us; the *Ganges, Monarch*, and *Defiance* a-head; the distance between each not exceeding a half cable. The judgement with which each ship calculated her station in that intricate Channel, was admirable throughout. The failure of the three Ships that were aground, and whose force was to have been opposed to the Trekroner battery, left his day, as glorious for seamanship as for courage, incomplete. The lead was in many Ships confided to the Master alone; and the contest that arose on board the *Elephant*, which of the two Officers who attended the heaving of it should stand in the larboard chains, was a noble competition, and greatly pleased the heart of Nelson, as he paced the quarter-deck. The gallant Riou, perceiving the blank in the original plan for the attack of the Crown Battery, proceeded down the Line with his Squadron of Frigates, and attempted, but in vain to fulfil the duty of the absent Ships of the Line. His force was unequal to it; and the general signal of recall, which was made about mid-action by the Commander-in-Chief, had the good effect of, at least, saving Riou's squadron from destruction.

About one PM few if any of the Enemy's heavy ships and Praams had ceased to fire. The *Isis* had greatly suffered by the superior weight of the *Provestein*'s fire; and if it had not been for the judicious diversion of it by the *Desirée*, Captain Inman, who raked her, and for other assistance from the *Polyphemus*, the Isis would have been destroyed. Both the *Isis* and *Bellona* had received serious injury by the bursting of some of their guns. The *Monarch* was also suffering severely under the united fire of the *Holstein* and *Zealand*; and only two of our Bomb-vessels would get to their station on the Middle Ground, and open their mortars on the Arsenal, directing their shells over both Fleets. Our Squadron of Gun-brigs, impeded by currents, could not, with the exception of one, although commanded by Captain Rose in the *Jamaica*, weather the eastern end of the Middle Ground, or come into Action. The Division of the Commander-in-Chief acted according to the preconcerted plan; but could only menace the entrance of the Harbour. The *Elephant* was warmly engaged by the *Dannebrog*, and by two heavy Praams on her bow and quarter. Signals of distress were on board the *Bellona* and *Russell*, and of inability from the *Agamemnon.* The contest, in general, although from the relaxed state of the Enemy's fire, it might not have given much room for apprehension as to the result, had certainly, at one PM not declared itself in favour of either side. About this juncture, and in this posture of affairs, the signal was thrown out on board the London, for action to cease.

Lord Nelson was at this time, as he had been during the whole Action, walking the starboard side of the quarter-deck; sometimes much animated, and at other heroically fine in his observations. A shot through the mainmast knocked a few splinters about us. He observed to me, with a smile, 'It is warm work, and this day may be the last to any of us at a moment;' and then stopping short at the gangway, he used an expression never to be erased from my memory, and said with emotion, 'but mark you, I would not be elsewhere for thousands.' When the signal, No.39, was made, the Signal Lieutenant reported it to him. He continued his walk, and did not appear to take notice of it. The Lieutenant meeting his Lordship at the next turn asked, 'whether he should repeat it?' Lord Nelson answered, 'No acknowledge it.' On the Officer returning to the poop, his Lordship called after him, 'Is No. 16 still hoisted?' the Lieutenant answering in the affirmative, Lord Nelson said, 'Mind you keep it so.' He now walked the deck considerably agitated, which was always known by his moving the stump of his right arm. After a turn or two, he said to me, in a quick manner, 'Do you know what's shown on board of the Commander-in-Chief, No. 39?' On asking him what that meant, he answered, 'Why, to leave off action!' he repeated, and then added, with a shrug, 'Now, damn me if I do'. He also observed, I believe, to Captain Foley, 'You know, Foley, I have only one eye – I have a right to be blind sometimes;' and then with an archness peculiar to his character, putting the glass to his blind eye, he exclaimed, 'I really do not see the signal.' This remarkable signal was, therefore, only acknowledged on board the *Elephant*, not repeated. Admiral Graves did the latter, not being able to distinguish the *Elephant*'s conduct; either by a fortunate accident, or intentionally, No. 16 was not displaced. The Squadron of Frigates obeyed the signal, and hauled off. That brave Officer, Captain Riou, was killed by a raking shot, when the *Amazon* showed her stern to the Trekroner. He was sitting on a gun, was encouraging his men, and had been wounded in the head by a splinter. He had expressed himself grieved at being thus obliged to retreat, and nobly observed, 'What will Nelson think of us?' His Clerk was killed by his side; and by another shot, several of the Marines, while hauling on the main-brace, shared the same fate. Riou then exclaimed, 'Come then, my boys, let us die all together!' The words were scarcely uttered, when the fatal shot severed him in two. Thus, and in an instant, was the British service deprived of one of its greatest ornaments, and society of a character of singular worth, resembling the heroes of romance.

The action now continued with unabated vigour. About two pm the greater part of the Danish line had ceased to fire; some of the lighter Ships were adrift, and the carnage on board of the Enemy, who reinforced their crews from the Shore, was dreadful. The taking possession of such Ships as had struck, was, however, attended with difficulty; partly by reason of the batteries of Amak Island protecting them, and partly because an irregular fire was made on our Boats, as they approached, from the Ships themselves. The *Dannebrog* acted in this manner, and fired at our boat, although the Ships was not only on fire and had struck, but the Commodore, Fischer, had removed his Pendant, and had deserted her. A renewed attack on her by the *Elephant* and *Glatton*, for a quarter of an hour, not only completely silenced and disabled the *Dannebrog*, but, by the use of grape, nearly killed every man who was in the Praams, ahead and astern of the unfortunate Ship. On our smoke clearing away, the *Dannebrog* was found to be drifting in flames before the wind, spreading terror throughout the Enemy's line. The usual lamentable scene then ensued; and our Boats rowed in every direction, to save the crew, who were throwing themselves from her at every port-hole; few, however, were left unwounded in her after our last broadsides, or could be saved. She drifted leeward and about half-past three blew up. The time of half-past two, brings me to a most important part of Lord Nelson's conduct on this day, and about which so much discussion has arisen: his sending a Flag of Truce on shore. To the best of my recollection, the facts were as follow. After the *Dannebrog* was adrift, and had ceased to fire, the Action was found to be over, along the whole of the Line astern of us; but not so with the Ships ahead and with the Crown batteries. Whether from ignorance of the custom of war, or from confusion on board the Prizes, our Boats were, as before mentioned, repulsed from the Ships themselves, or fired at from Amak Island. Lord Nelson naturally lost temper at this, and observed, 'That he must either send on shore, and stop this irregular proceedings, or send in our Fire-ships and burn them.' He accordingly retired into the stern gallery, and wrote, with great dispatch, that well-known Letter (see below) addressed to the Crown Prince, with the address, 'To the Brothers of Englishmen, the brave Danes, &c;' and this Letter was conveyed on shore through the contending Fleets by Captain Sir Frederick

Thesiger, who acted as his Lordship's Aid-de-camp; and found the Prince near the Sally-port, animating his people in a spirited manner.'

[Breaking into Colonel Stewart's narrative:-
Nelson was as usual on deck walking and intermittently talking to his officers. Also present and free to move about were Danish lieutenant prisoners of war who were able to observe the conduct of affairs at close quarters. Amongst the tumult and confusion of the battle, exposed on the deck of the Elephant, Nelson was seen to write his now famous note using the rudderhead as a desk. Captain Foley watched as Nelson wrote and his Secretary Thomas Wallis copied - it was dated 2nd April on board the *Elephant*, addressed to 'The Brothers of Englishmen The Danes' and read:- 'Lord Nelson has directions to spare Denmark when no longer resisting but if the firing is continued on the part of Denmark Lord Nelson will be obliged to set on fire all the floating batteries he has taken, without having the power of saving the brave Danes who have defended them'.
The note is marked by ink but clearly legible and as it was about to be sealed by a wafer of wax Nelson insisted that it be properly secured with wax embossed by his seal 'or the enemy will think it has been written and sent in a hurry'. A man was sent to his cabin but was killed crossing the deck and a second had to be sent to collect the wax and Nelson's seal which was duly applied to complete the dispatch.]
Captain Sir Frederick Thesiger, who spoke Danish and Russian, volunteered to make the hazardous journey under a flag of truce in the gig from the *Elephant*. Those defenders who saw the flag allowed the vessel to pass without hindrance but in the fury of the battle much shot and debris was flying about and they were fortunate to reach the Danish *Elephanten* unharmed and from there were piloted into the harbour. The Crown Prince was at the jetty observing the course of the battle and, from the North, the approach of Sir Hyde Parker's division. From this position he had seen the increasing number of casualties being landed and had received, directly, the reports from his brave captains, who described their experiences and the reduction of the defences. After discussion with his Defence Commission, Captain Lindholm, who spoke English, was directed to represent the Crown Prince in establishing with Nelson exactly what was being offered. In the meantime Nelson was

considering taking advantage of the wind to ease the able capital ships further north in the direction of the harbour entrance. Captain Lindholm presented the Crown Prince's query directly to Nelson who asked that it be written down then wrote immediately:-

'Lord Nelson's object in sending on shore a Flag of Truce is humanity; he therefore consents that hostilities shall cease till Lord Nelson can take his prisoners out of the Prizes, and he consents to land all the wounded Danes, and to burn or remove his prizes.

Lord Nelson, with humble duty to His Royal Highness, begs leave to say that he will ever esteem it the greatest victory he ever gained if his Flag of Truce may be the happy forerunner of a lasting and happy union between my most gracious Sovereign and his Majesty the King of Denmark.'

Soon after the gig completed the return journey to the jetty and the Crown Prince firing from the batteries ceased and the flag of truce was hoisted on the *Elephant* and noted on the *London* at 3.15pm. As they cut their anchors to leave the hazards of the channel the *Elephant* and *Defiance* temporarily grounded on the shoals. In an endeavour to save lives from the burning *Dannebrog*, launches were sent from the *Ardent* and *Glatton*, recovering many Danish survivors before she exploded. The *Elephant* grounded, Nelson arrived briefly on the *London* as his Commander-in-Chief was dealing with the details of the truce through Captain Lindholm, then left for his cabin on the S*t. George.*

Returning to the narrative of Colonel Stewart:-

'Whether we were actually firing at that time in the *Elephant* or not, I am unable to recollect; it could only have been partially, at such of the farther Ships as had not struck. The three Ships ahead of us were, however, engaged; and from the superiority of the force opposed to them, it was by no means improbable the Lord Nelson's observing eye pointed out to him the expediency of a prudent conduct. Whether this suggested to him the policy of a Flag of Truce, or not, two solid reasons were apparent, and were such as to justify the measure; viz., the necessity of stopping the irregular fire from the Ships which had surrendered – and the singular opportunity that was thus given, of sounding the feelings of an Enemy, who had reluctantly entered into the war, and who must feel the generosity of the first offer of amity coming from a conquering foe. If there were a third reason for the conduct of the noble Admiral, and some of his own Officers assert this, it was unnecessary that it should have been expressed; it was certainly not avowed, and will for ever remain a matter of conjecture. While the Boat was absent, the animated fire of the Ships ahead of us, and the approach of two of the Commander-in-Chief's division, the *Ramilies* and *Defence*, caused the remainder of the Enemy's line to the eastward of the Trekroner to strike: that formidable Work continued its fire, but fortunately at too long a range to do serious damage to any one except the *Monarch*, whose loss in men, this day, exceeded that of any Line-of-Battle ship during the war. From the uninjured state of this Outwork, which had been manned at the close of the Action with nearly 1500 men, it was deemed impracticable to carry into execution the projected plan for storming it; the Boats for this service had been on the starboard side of each Ship during the Action. The firing from the Crown Battery and from our leading Ships did not cease until past three o'clock, when the Danish Adjutant-General, Lindholm, returning with a Flag of Truce, directed the fire of the battery to be suspended. The signal for doing the same, on our part, was made from our Ship to those engaged. The Action closed after five hour's duration, four of which were warmly contested.

The answer from the Prince Regent was to inquire more minutely into the purport of the message. I should here observe, that previous to the Boat's getting on board, Lord Nelson had taken the opinion of his valuable friends, Fremantle and Foley, the former of whom had been sent for from the *Ganges*, as to the practicability of advancing with the Ships which were least damaged, upon that part of the Danish Line of Defence yet uninjured. Their opinions were averse from it; and, on the other hand, decided in favour of removing our Fleet, whilst the wind yet held fair, from their present intricate Channel. .... His Lordship, having finished his letter (to the Crown Prince), referred the Adjutant-General to the Commander-in-Chief, who was at anchor at least four miles off, for a conference on the important points which the latter part of the message had alluded to; and to this General Lindholm did not object, but proceeded to the *London*. Lord Nelson wisely foresaw, that, exclusive of the valuable opportunity that now offered itself for a renewal of Peace, time would be gained by this long row out to sea, for our leading Ships, which were much crippled, to clear the shoals, and whose course was under the immediate fire of the Trekroner. The Adjutant-General was no sooner gone to the *London*, and Captain Thesiger despatched on shore than the signal was made for the *Glatton, Elephant, Ganges, Defiance*, and *Monarch*, to weigh in succession. The intricacy of the Channel now showed the great utility of what had been done; the *Monarch* as first Ship, immediately hit on a shoal, but was pushed over it by the *Ganges* taking her amid-ships. The *Glatton* went clear, but the *Defiance* and *Elephant* ran aground, leaving the Crown Battery at a mile distance; and there they remained fixed, the former until ten o'clock that night , and the latter until eight, notwithstanding every exertion which their fatigued crews could make to relieve them. Had there been no cessation of hostilities, their situation would certainly have been perilous; but it should be observed, on the other hand, that measures would in that case have been adopted, and they were within our power, for destroying this formidable Work.

The *Elephant* being aground, Lord Nelson followed the Adjutant-General, about four o'clock, to the *London*, where the negotiation first began, which terminated in an honourable Peace. He was low in spirits at the surrounding scene of devastation, and particularly felt for the blowing up of the *Dannebrog*. 'Well' he exclaimed, 'I have fought contrary to orders, and I shall perhaps be hanged; never mind, let them.' Lindholm returned to Copenhagen the same evening, when it was agreed that all Prizes should be surrendered, and the suspension of hostilities continue for twenty-four hours; the whole of the Danish wounded were to be received on shore. Lord Nelson then repaired on board the *St. George*, and the night was actively passed by the Boats of the Division which had not been engaged, in getting afloat the Ships that were ashore, and in bringing out the Prizes. The *Desirée* frigate, towards the close of the Action, going to the aid of the *Bellona* became fast on the same shoal; but neither these Ships, nor the *Russell*, were in any danger from the Enemy's batteries, as the world has frequently since been led to suppose.'

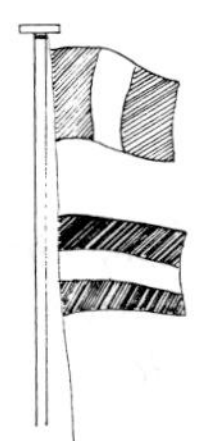

[THE SIGNAL SAGA]

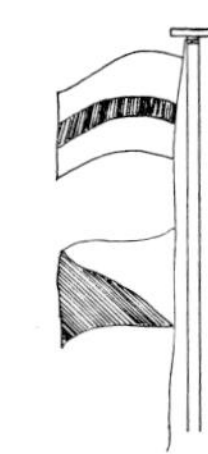

Commander Bruce Nicolls OBE RN (Retd)
Vexillographer
Flag Consultant and Designer

It would not have been at all surprising if, next to his favourite signal, No 16, ENGAGE THE ENEMY MORE CLOSELY, the signal most indelibly printed on Nelson's mind after the Battle of Copenhagen was its complete opposite, the one sent by his Commander in Chief, the one that nearly caused the battle to be lost, No 39, DISCONTINUE THE ACTION. The arguments over Admiral Parker's action are covered elsewhere in this book, and need not concern us here.

Fortunately, Nelson had hoisted No 16 as the battle commenced and, as he did at Trafalgar, kept it flying, so it was still flying when No 39 was hoisted, as a general signal to all ships, by the Commander in Chief. It could well be argued that this practice of Nelson's saved the day.

Rear Admiral Graves, next in the line of command to Nelson, had no doubt about which signal should be obeyed. It was his duty to repeat No 39, but he ignored it for as long as possible, and when he did repeat it, hoisted it where Nelson could not see it. At the same time, he kept No 16 flying, clearly indicating his view on the matter.

The conflict of conscience caused some Captains to begin withdrawing from the battle, but for most there was no doubt. As did Nelson, they turned a blind eye to the Commander in Chief's signal, and followed Nelson's familiar exhortation to engage the enemy more closely. They knew, as did their hero, that they were about to win the battle.

Signally speaking, the Battle of Copenhagen was significant not only because of Hyde Parker's controversial order, but because it was the first major battle fought using the Admiralty "Signal Book for the Ships of War" introduced in 1799. This book did not differ greatly from Admiral Lord Howe's signal book of 1790, but it marked the culmination of centuries of development, and provided the system on which naval signal codes were based from then on.

The flags used in the Admiralty book were mostly the same as in Howe's book. One of the few changes was to the Flag 1, which had previously been a plain red flag, so Nelson's favourite signal No 16 was changed. A further change in the number of the flags, but not the flags themselves, was made in 1803, when a copy of the Signal Book fell into French hands. Thus the flags of the No 16 signal that Nelson flew at Trafalgar differed from those flown at Copenhagen.

THE BATTLE OF COPENHAGEN ROADS

THE TRANSCRIPTION OF A TALK BY CAPTAIN FINN VOLKE
COMMANDING OFFICER COPENHAGEN NAVAL BASE
JUNE 1990

During the 18th century Denmark had enjoyed the longest period of peace in her history. By not taking either side in the European conflict, Denmark intended to capitalise on her position by shipping and trading under the neutral flag. This created problems, which eventually led to the battle of Copenhagen. It was however not Denmark's battle, but part of the major powers' fight for control of Europe. Until 1797 Denmark had been rather successful in maintaining a defensive neutral policy, but after that year, the year when our great politician A.B. Bernstorff died the policy changed to an offensive one with Denmark escorting convoys with men of war.

British Ultimatum

The Danish Escort Force Commanders were under no circumstances to allow visitation of the convoys, and their orders forced the British to send an ultimatum to the Danish Government:

1. To allow British visitation of the convoys;
2. To cancel the escort force commander's orders to stop the convoy system until negotiations between the two governments about agreements and about principles for neutral convoys had taken place.

The result of this was in short, that Denmark at the end of 1800 was forced into the Neutrality Alliance with Russia, Sweden, and Prussia, not knowing that the Russian Tsar had already commenced negotiations with France.

Neutrality Alliance and State of War

But England at the beginning of December 1800 had already decided to make war with the members of the Neutrality Alliance and was planning a naval intrusion in the Baltic. Vice Admiral Sir Hyde Parker was the British Naval Officer with the most thorough knowledge of the Baltic so he was chosen to be the Commanding Officer of the Baltic Squadron and Lord Nelson was appointed his executive officer. I shall not go into details about all the difficulties to get underway, nor Lord Nelson's impatience, but by the 22nd of March 1801 the British Baltic Squadron was at anchor just off Kullen awaiting the answer to the British ultimatum to the Danish Government. The squadron consisted of twenty ships of the line and nearly double the number of smaller ships. The ultimatum, which the British Envoy presented, was an agreement with the Danes concerning the principles of neutrality and free passage for the Royal Navy through the Danish Straits. If accepted, England would sign a defence alliance with Denmark. The answer was given within eight hours. The ultimatum was sent on the evening of the 20th March and the answer was given in the morning of the 21st. It was a blank refusal, and with the answer was the envoy's passport. So from that moment there was a state of war between England and Denmark.

Danish Preparations

At the beginning of 1801 when war was drawing nearer there was pressure on the Naval Bases on Copenhagen. First, ten ships of the line were to be equipped for the Neutrality Alliance, second the seaward defence of Copenhagen was to be established and later on at a request from Norway a squadron of two ships of the line and two frigates had to be made ready for sea as soon as possible. It was an overwhelming job and the Norwegian squadron was not ready for sea, when intelligence reported the British fleet at anchor off Kullen. So the Squadron remained in Copenhagen.

The plan was to have the not yet finished fortress the Trekroner in the north end, and in the south entrance to Kongedybet three old ships of the line were grounded to form a fortress. In between the northern and southern forts a floating defence consisted of twelve ships or barges in two lines, all anchored or moored. The entrance to the Harbour was defended from the Trekroner and two old ships the *Mars* and the *Elefanten*. But it took time to get things organised. First the equipping of the ships with unskilled crews. All the professional sailors were on board the squadrons, which were to be defended or away on convoy duties. After completing their equipment the ships and barges had to warp out through the heavy ice and into their positions. If Admiral Parker could have made up his mind and proceeded down the Sound without delay; he would have found a defence in a total mess. The wind was an ally for the Danes and gave them the much needed time to get the defence line established, and moreover it gave some of the crews a chance to get organised and trained with the guns. The crews, I have already mentioned, were rather mixed.

Manning the defences

Every ship and barge had a Naval Officer as Commanding Officer, but a lot of the other officers were from the merchant navy or midshipmen with no battle experience. The private sailors were either conscripts from all over Denmark and Norway, a lot of them had never been on board a ship before, or they were sailors from the merchant navy who of course had a maritime background, but no battle experience. Then of course there were the petty officers and the skeleton crew, which were the nucleus but they were few, for instance 30% of the gunners mates were missing. A rather large amount of conscripts came from Norway. They were all very much wanted as they had some experience all being sailors or fishermen. To get them to Copenhagen they were marched down through Sweden. Equipped with a new pair of shoes at the start. They marched forty kilometres a day over nine days with a rest day every third day and 1561 trained Norwegian sailors reached Copenhagen that way and were divided between the squadron and the seaward defence ships.

Volunteers

There were also volunteers. On the 20th March 2054 men out of the 5000 required were still needed to man the defence ships. The Admiralty sent out an appeal for volunteers, and nearly 2000 answered the appeal but of course, most of them had no experience. It was a mixed group. Most welcome were the sixty-one sailors from the merchant navy, and a group of Indian sailors with their leaders. Seventeen per cent of the volunteers were from Sweden. But other foreigners volunteered – two Russians, two Italians – one from Spain – a French umbrella maker and a man from Cape of Good Hope. But of course one might question the quality. It was the responsibility of the Admiralty to furnish the crews and they succeeded.

Organising the Defence

The Commanding Officer Captain Olfert Fischer distributed the crews in accordance with his plans and anticipations. The frigate *Elven* had a complete professional crew because she was the signal relay ship and needed to be able to manoeuvre fast and exactly. The *Dannebrog* had not one volunteer or pressed man onboard; the crew consisted of professional sailors. She was the command platform and therefore should be able last out the longest. Olfert Fischer had for the rest of the line divided the crews from the anticipation that the British would attack from the north. Therefore the northernmost ships had the best or most professional crews, while the southernmost had the volunteers and the pressed men. The Commanding Officer was very busy getting the defence ships on station and duly trained. He was working day and night, and signals were sent out from the command ship. But not all of them were understood as most of the subordinate officers had no experience or knowledge of signalling, and if they did not understand the signals – they did not know what orders to pass on. But communication was not the only problem. The gun crews had little or no experience, and there was little time to train them in the procedures in the handling of the guns. Therefore gunners from the naval arsenal were sent onboard the ships to train the crews, but with orders to leave the ships -–when action commenced. But it proved difficult to make them leave and most of them asked permission to stay on board and they were a great help during the battle. As one of the gunners later said, what was he to tell his fourteen-year-old son, who was a powder boy in the arsenal, if he had gone ashore when the enemy came? It was hard work, and to many completely new to learn the right procedures for handling the guns. Any spare time was taken to practice gun handling. But there was much more to be done. Not all the guns had gun carriages. The naval arsenal was working around the clock to make carriages and in the evening of the 29th of March a barge came warping out with the seventeen slide-carriages and distributed them to different ships. Powder was to be fetched from the magazines at the Fortress Kastellet, and every night all ships were in first degree of readiness against surprise attacks, especially from fire ships.

‘Guns Free’

At five o’clock that morning the northernmost ships the *Elefanten* was ordered to “stay alert”, and at the same time a liaison officer from the squadron which was ready for Norway by now, was called on board the *Dannebrog.* At 0545 action stations was ordered at the defence line, and when the cannonade from *Kronborg* had lasted for half an hour, Olfert Fischer gave the order “Guns free”. Now the British came. First the Danish *Nidelven*, who as a scout had observed the Baltic fleet north of Kronborg came soaring with all sails set and with the British Jack on the foretop and constantly firing her signal guns. At eight o’clock lieutenant Willemoes with *Flådebatteri* No. 1 was ordered to take up position between the *Sjælland* and the *Dannebrog*. At nine o’clock he was in position and at ten o’clock the first British ships anchored in Copenhagen Roads. At last the waiting time was over, only the artilleribarge *Hajen* missing, but underway to take up her position. But where were the allies?

Denmark’s Allies?

First France. They had in the beginning expressed Latin enthusiasm with a lot of words and gestures and that was all. Prussia and Denmark were not on a friendly footing, and had done nothing to establish friendly connections, so no help from them, and they had no navy anyway. And the Russian Navy was very conveniently icebound – so there was no reason to look for the Tsar’s Navy. Then there was only the Swedish Navy to hope for, but Denmark and Sweden had been arch enemies for centuries, and now we were members of the same alliance. Did we really rely on them? So far the negotiations had not brought any reason to believe in them, but when the Swedish King Gustav IV Adolf from Helsingborg had witnessed how the British fleet had sailed past the fortress Kronborg, he decided to let the Karlskrona squadron go to the assistance of the Danish defence. On 31st of March it was agreed, that the Swedish squadron of seven ships of the line and three frigates, should take position south of the Danish line across the Kongedybet. With the Swedish reinforcement the number of guns would be almost doubled. But the wind which formerly had been an ally for the Danes had changed sides, and the south wind which helped Nelson up through Kongedybet – made it impossible for the Swedish ships to clear Karlskrona's skerries. And even if they had been able to clear the skerries, they were too late.

The eve of battle

On the 1st April Nelson had outmanoeuvred the Swedes and placed his squadron south of the Middelgrund between the Swedes and the Danes. Being members of the Nelson Society I am sure that you have studied the battle and know every move, so I will try to give the Danish Version. During Nelson's passage of Hollænderdybet, Olfert Fischer had observed the British fleet – but as the distance was too great, he was not able to interfere. All his ships were at anchor in the defence line and with the British fleet just north of the Middelgrund it would have been a rather desperate undertaking to let the squadron in Kronløbet interfere, or let the gunboat flotilla run out. Then again he did of course not know the British plan. Maybe the British were going into the Baltic, and if so there was no reason to provoke an attack. The small gunbarge *Hajen* reached the last position, and now the line was complete. In the evening of the 1st April Nelson's Squadron was at anchor south of the Middelgrund and in a right formation. Lieutenant Stricker, who was in command of the battery at Amager, asked for permission to use his mortars to shell the British ships. In the evening after dark he obtained the permission and three shells were fired, but the colonel who was in charged of the artillericorps got the impression that the ships were outside mortar range, so he ordered a cease fire. But from the *Hajen* they observed the shells to fall in between the ships, and onboard the British ships it created some concern and great surprise when the shelling stopped. But the colonel not having the observations from the *Hajen* unfortunately ordered the battery to stop firing.

'Action Stations'

The next morning when dawn broke the first signal went up onboard the Danish command ship the *Dannebrog:* ACTION STATIONS. It was not really necessary, because onboard all the ships the crews had been ready all night long, and as soon as the wind had turned to the south – everybody knew what that meant and what was coming. Onboard the gunbarge *Hajen* the commander, Lieutenant Müller realized, that if his crew should have a change it was not food they needed, it was practice, and that morning the untrained crew of artisans and soldiers got their first and only lecture in how to handle the guns – and then it was time for breakfast. Captain Risbrick, on the *Wagrien*, who during the American Liberty War, had served in the Royal Navy observed the activity within Nelson's Squadron and understood the signs. Having observed the *Elephant* with the Vice Admiral's flag he turned to his officers and said: 'Gentlemen – now they are weighing to attack us. Let us have lunch – we will have a busy day'. Olfert Fischer repeated his signal and ordered his ships to be ready to take the attack from the south. To the north you could see Parker's ships weighing and take a southerly course towards Copenhagen. At 10.15 the signal "Guns free" was hoisted onboard the Danish ships.

'Open Fire'

The *Prøvestenen* the southernmost ships was the first to open fire. At 1030 Lieutenant Bille fired the first shot to open the battle. Captain Murray onboard the *Edgar* answered the fire, while manoeuvring to his planned position leading the British line into Kongedybet. From the Danish line, there was little to be seen through the gunsmoke, as the British ships proceeded in formation with thundering guns up along the Danish line until they reached their appointed positions, where they anchored and concentrated against their designated opponents. At eleven o'clock all the British capital ships were engaged in the fighting. Only the three northernmost Danish ships the *Holsten* – the *Infødstretten* and the *Hjælperen* were not engaged yet. The *Prøvestenen* had exchanged fire with all the British ships as they turned into Konedybet. But now she was left with her own opponents the *Polyphemus* – the *Russell* and the thirty-six gun frigate *Desireé,* which was able to direct her fire to rake the *Rendsborg*, *Wagrien* and the *Prøvestenen* without any of them being able to return the fire.

Therefore Captain Lassen concentrated on the *Polyphemus* and the *Russell* hoping that the battery at Amager – the Strickers Battery – could do something about the frigate. The *Wagrien*'s main opponent was the *Isis* and she was rather close, but she was not alone. The grounded *Bellona* was rather a nuisance too. Therefore Captain Risbrick who was aware of the British superiority instructed his gunners to aim at the hulls to disrupt the guns. The *Rendsborg* and the *Nyborg* which originally were barges for cavalry horses and *Jylland* had felt the war machine pass by before they could concentrate against their targets, and the small barge *Sværdfisken* was almost shot out of the water, but the Norwegian crew fought back the best they could. They had not marched all the way down from Norway for nothing!

Attrition

The *Dannebrog*, which flew the command pennant was the prime target and drew much fire away from the smaller ships the *Hajen* – the frigate *Elven* – the Kronborg – the Aggerhus and Willemoes' the *Flådebatteri No. 1*. North of the Danish centre the *Sjælland* – the *Charlotte Amalie* and the *Søhesten* were engaged. Especially the *Charlotte Amalie* which was an old merchant vessel – low in the water was under constant fire from the *Monarch*, and a detachment of twenty men and a petty officer were busy throwing the dead overboard or bringing wounded down to the sickbay. At 1115 the *Rendsborg* had to leave her position. A cannonball hit in the forward part of the ship and gave her a serious leak and parted the anchor cable, so she turned her stern towards the enemy. A rather unhealthy position. Therefore the Commanding Officer Lieutenant Commander Egede had no choice: He let go his other anchor and manoeuvred with the sails. He grounded her in a way so that he could still use her guns. But he left a gap in the line. From that position he continued fighting until he had to give in at 1500. It was a dangerous situation which fortunately could not be exploited by the British as their gunbrigs were still east of the Middlgrund, and the big ships of the line were unable to carry out complicated manoeuvres in unknown waters under heavy fire. But Captain Murray onboard the *Edgar* swung his bow to the west and was able to direct his fire at *Wagrien*'s port quarter, and Captain Risbrick who had enough to do with the *Isis* and the *Bellona* could do nothing about it. Captain Risbrick had hoped for support from the shore batteries, but the distance to the British ships was too great and though the batteries tried to shell the British line with mortars, and used the method of ricochet-firing to increase the range, they did not play any significant role in the battle. Neither did the gunboat flotilla. It was there and was to be used as a moving force to block the openings in the lines, but it was unprofessionally led, and as the battle developed communication from the command ship to the gunboats was impossible due to the heavy gunsmoke. So it was more or less each boat for itself taking shot on the British line.

Fischer moves his flag

The *Dannebroge*, as said, being the command ship was the capital target and the *Elephant* as well as the *Glatton* concentrated their fire against her. So after only half an hour Olfert Fischer realised that the ship could not stand much more – and transferred his command to the *Holsten*. The *Dannebrog* continued to fight back the British as well as a serious fire. With only three guns left the commanding officer decided to haul down the flag. He realised that he had nothing left to fight with and the fire was spreading. Therefore he concentrated on saving as many lives as possible At 1430 he ceased fire and later the *Dannebrog* started to drift north – with the current. At 1630 the ship blew up, almost as the *Dannebrog* a hundred years earlier in Køge Bugt. The *Elven,* the small frigate which was to act as signal relay station, had taken part in the battle with her ten guns. The *Elephant* and the *Glatton* were a bit too much for the small frigate, and she received a lot of damage to her mast and rigging. At 1230 the Commanding Officer of the *Elven* observed that the *Dannebrog*'s flag was missing and he believed that the *Dannebrog* had quit. It was not so – the flag he been shot down and was rehoisted, but at that time the *Elven* had gone. Next to withdraw was the horsebarge *Aggershus*, also in the vicinity of the *Dannebrog*. When the *Elephant* and the *Ganges* were within range the *Aggershus* commenced firing but one hour later she had only three usable guns left. With those three she continued for another hour, when one of the anchor cables was parted and she turned the stern towards the enemy. Now the commanding officer had no way to fight back, and decided to save the rest of his crew. But how was the question? His ship was badly shot up and only a demolished wreck. The sistership *Nyborg*, which had been just as badly damaged and only had one gun left, drifted north with one sail. She succeeded in taking the *Aggershus* in tow and took the wounded on board. So the *Aggershus* was towed into the northern part of the harbour where she was scuttled. The *Nyborg* the saviour sank just north of the entrance to the naval base. But both ships sank flying the Danish Ensign.

Flådebatteri No.1

The Flådebatteri No. 1, which was only a flat barge with twenty guns without any shelter or cover, had two impressive opponents the *Elephant* and the *Ganges* and though they had concentrated against the *Dannebrog* they had enough left to deal with a small barge. After one and a half hours there were forty-six killed and wounded. The seventeen year old commanding officer Lieutenant Willemoes, as he saw the *Aggershus* and the *Elven* withdraw realised he could do no more harm to the enemy and let go his moorings and drifted north, where he was picked up by boats from the ships in Kronløbet. Just north of the *Dannebrog* was the *Sjælland*, a seventy four gun ship with full crew. Originally Nelson had chosen the *Sjælland* as his opponent, but as he had to change plans at the last moment, the *Monarch* and the *Ganges* got the job. About eleven o'clock the *Sjælland* opened fire, but the *Ganges* and *Monarch* were too much for her and after two hours there was hardly a usable gun left. She had received so many waterline hits, that she was in danger of sinking. So the Commanding Officer, Captain Harboe gave the order to cut the cables as he hoped to drift into shallow water south of the fortress Trekroner. But as he later realised, he would drift into the firing line of the guns from the fortress he reanchored, and with some of the survivors he continued to fire back with what was left. But about 1400 Captain Harboe decided to haul down the flag and throw everything overboard.

Centre of the defensive line

In the centre of the Danish line not much was left. The *Elven* was gone and so was the *Aggershus* – the *Flådebatteri No. 1* and the *Sjælland*. The *Dannebrog* still returned fire but with greater and greater intervals and the fire onboard was rapidly spreading. But still the centre was fighting. The small barge *Hajen* was

rather unimpresssed by the fifty-eight gun ship *Glatton*. The artisans and the sailors had little experience in the handling of guns, but everybody from the Commanding Officer to the youngest were busy loading, aiming and firing. But they were running out of powder, so Lieutenant Müller hoisted the signal for more powder. But now all the big ships concentrated their fire on the *Hajen* and she had to give in. Lieutenant Müller hauled down the flag, but as the British ships continued to fire at him he sent the crew down below and then he himself with the gunners mate spiked the guns and tried to construct a raft to save his crew. It was about 1445 when two armed British boats brought him and his crew on board the *Elephant*, where he was presented to Nelson, who by that time had sent his envoy ashore, and he said to the young Lieutenant: "I am sorry of what has taken place today, and to prove it I have sent an envoy ashore to arrange a cease fire. Should however this be rejected I will have to take the Trekroner Battery and burn down the Arsenal".
Unimpressed the Lieutenant answered: "There are some circumstances about the Trekroner which you may not be aware of, and concerning the Arsenal my countrymen are not stupid to leave anything there, if you shell it". But of course the Admiral had no time to get into a discussion with the young sub-lieutenant. Now the fight in the centre was over, but it had lasted longer than Nelson had anticipated.

Northern defence joins the battle

Nelson's job was not to sink the Danish ships, but to take them and bring his own mortarships within range of Copenhagen and the Naval Base, but as long as he had not seized the Danish ships, he could not bring the mortarships into position, and as long as the Danish ships resisted the British boarding attempts, he was not able to fulfil his mission. And he still had to neutralise the northernmost ships. As Nelson had to improvise his plan, the northern ships first joined battle about one hour later than the rest. About eleven o'clock the *Charlotte Amalie* was engaged by the *Defiance*. Seventy-four guns against twenty-six, which was a rather uneven fight, but when the *Monarch* and *Ganges* could also concentrate against him, Captain Kofoed on the *Charlotte Amalie* realised it was a losing battle and decided to strike the flag and pennant. It was then 1445. As the British ships continued to fire upon him, he concentrated on saving as many men as possible and send them to the Trekroner where they could rejoin the battle. He managed to save one hundred and sixty-seven of the crew of two hundred and forty-one. Thirty-nine were killed and twenty-eight were taken prisoner, and seven just disappeared. At eleven o'clock the *Søhesten* a small barge joined the battle. For three and a half hours the crew handled the guns, reanchored the barge several times, and at last there were only two guns left. So at 1430 Lieutenant Middlebo realised that it was meaningless to continue, and he hauled down his flag, and shortly afterwards he and the survivors were taken away as prisoners.

Fischer transfers to the *Holsten*

Olfert Fischer at 1130 boarded the *Holsten* and made it his command ship and about twelve o'clock the *Defiance* with Rear Admiral Graves left the *Charlotte Amelia* to the *Ganges* and paid out on his anchor cable and manoeuvred alongside the *Holsten*, and for them the waiting time was over. But on the *Holsten* they had not been passive. Due to the heavy gunsmoke they could not see the enemy, but sometimes they saw a cannonball or the flashes from the cannons and though the distance was rather great they elevated the guns and aimed in that direction. The *Defiance* with her seventy-four guns was rather superior to the sixty gun Danish ship and the quick and precise shooting from the British ship damaged the *Holsten* so much in one hour and forty-five minutes, that Olfert Fischer once again had to change his command position. This time to the Trekroner Fortress. But the *Holsten* continued fighting for forty-five minutes after Olfert Fischer had to leave her. The Captain Arenfeldt realised that he could do no more with what he had left, and hauled down the flag at 1430. Shortly afterwards Captain Arenfeldt and his crew were taken prisoner and taken to the London.

The next morning some of the Danish wounded had died and Captain Arenfeldt on board the *London* performed the Danish naval ritual for burial at sea. One ship did not follow the example of the rest. The frigate *Hjælperen*, which was a specially constructed ship left the battle after only one hour and with rather minor material damage and a few wounded. What made the captain take this decision, we will never know but his explanation was, that when he saw the condition of the defence line, he realised that he could do nothing and then he left.

The *Infødsretten* was with the rest of the northernmost ships, without any knowledge of what was going on at the southern end and in the centre, but around one o'clock some of the Danish ships and barges came by, and gave a better impression of what had been going on down there. But *Infødsretten* did not get much time to worry because now the British frigates came up and took up their positions and her battle began. Half an hour later the Commanding Officer Captain Thurah was killed, and another half an hour later the executive officer was killed too. Now there was no one in charge and everything was confusion onboard.
A boat was sent to the Naval Base to report the situation, and Captain Schrödersee, who was a member of the train of attendants of the Crown Prince and as such witnessed the ongoing battle from the Sixtus Battery, volunteered to take charge of the ship. Together with some other volunteers from the Naval Base he boarded the *Infødsretten*. Shrödersee was killed the instant he set foot on the deck, and the volunteers found a disorganised ship. It was fired upon alongships which made it impossible to swing the ship, to get the guns to bear on the enemy. At 1500 the flag was hauled down after the guns had been demolished and the ammunition thrown overboard. The volunteers then left the wreck and continued to the *Elefanten* to assist there, should she join the battle. But they never came into action. Though some of Admiral Parker's ships opened fire, and the *Mars* and the *Elefanten* returned the fire, they never took part in the battle, and the same applied to the Squadron anchored up in Kronløbet. Now at 1500 the centre and the north were silenced. But there was still fighting in the south, and the resistance there was tough.

<u>Resistance of the Southern defence</u>
When the *Rendsborg* and the *Nyborg* withdrew they left a serious gap in the line and the southern defence was divided into two parts. The *Jylland* had the *Edgar* as her opponent and the latter's guns created havoc onboard the Danish ship. After about four hours the *Jylland* had only four guns left and to save the rest of the crew

Captain Brandt hauled down his flag and cut his anchor cables to drift in on the Refshalegrund. He still had some of the crew left and they were sent with the executive officer to the *Rendesborg* but she was just as demolished – so he decided to go on to the fortress. The Commanding Officer stayed onboard to take care of the wounded, but was taken prisoner and taken to the *Ardent*. The *Kronborg* and the *Sværdfisken* were just as tough as the *Jylland*, though they were smaller and had a weaker armament. The *Kronborg* was the smallest ship in the line with only twenty-two guns and the *Sværdfisken* was a barge with eighteen guns and almost no protection. But the *Sværdfisken* fought the best she could until she had only one gun left, then she had to give in. But nothing fell into enemy hands – what was still usable was thrown overboard. The *Kronborg* fought just as bravely, and when they had no more guns left, they threw the ammunition overboard and hauled down the flag. But still the horsebarge the *Rendsborg* aground on the Refshalegrunden was firing and she continued until she was completely demolished. At 1500 Lieutenant Commander Egede threw what was left of ammunition (forty-nine shots) and his signal books overboard and hauled down the flag. But due to the position five hundred to six hundred metres behind the line they succeeded in saving more than half the crew. Now only the *Wagrien* and the *Prøvestenen* were fighting, and they had their hands full. The *Isis*, the *Polyphemus*, the *Bellona* and the *Russell*, the frigate *Desireé* and now came the four gunbrigs, which had a hard fight against wind and current to clear the Middelgrund. *Wagrien* had much better trained gunners than the *Prøvestenen* and Captain Risbrick had war experience from serving in the Royal Navy. But against superior force, it was a question of time and when he had only three guns left he could do no more, except try to save as many as possible from being taken prisoner. He demolished the guns, threw the ammunition overboard, left the doctors on board to take care of the wounded and having finished all those preparations at 1515, he set off for land with those able to come along.

Ceasefire

Now only the *Prøvestenen* was flying the Danish ensign. The *Prøvestenen* had a bad day with just as many opponents as the *Wagrien*. Three times the ship was on fire. The flag was shot down twice and the Command pennant once and as the shelling with anti-personnel grenades caused heavy losses among the crew on the upper deck, Captain Lasen ordered them down below to reinforce the guncrews there. On the *Prøvestenen* as well as on the other ships there was that day a lot of people who performed far more than their duties – but it would take too long to mention them. As Captain Lassen saw the boats pull away from the *Wagrien* and as he only had two guns left, he gave the order to cease fire, and the last Danish gun fired from the defence line was fired by a Norwegian sailor. Captain Lassen left with who were able to go with him, while Lieutenant Michael Bille, who opened the battle stayed on board to keep up the morale of those who could not go. The battle was over and it was lost.

Olfert Fischer's mission was to keep control of Kongedybet to prevent the British mortarships taking up shelling positions. Now the mortars were there. The aim of Parker and Nelson was to gain control of the sound area, thus being able to threaten a bombardment of Copenhagen and force Denmark out of the alliance, and now it was all up to the politicians. Lord Nelson was impressed by the bravery of the Danish officers and men and during the negotiations following the battle he said to the Crown Prince, talking about the young officer Willemoes, commanding the Flådebatteri No.1 that he deserved to be made an Admiral for his bravery.
The Crown Prince answered: "Should I reward my brave officers as they deserved there would be no Captains or Lieutenants left in my Navy!".

DANISH UNITS

NORTHWING						
TYPE	NAME	STATUS	TIME	GUNS	DEAD	W'DED
FORT	TREKRONER			66	1	5
FREGAT	HJÆKOEREN	~	1300	16	0	6
BLOKSKIB	INDFØDSRETTEN	>	1500	64	21	41
LINIESKIB	HOLSTEN	>	1415	60	12	53
STYKPRAM	SØHESTEN	>	1430	18	12	21
BLOKSKIB	CH.AMALIE	>	1445	26	19	20
CENTRE			Subtotal	250	65	146
LINIESKIB	SJÆLLAND	>	1400	74	39	125
FLYDERBatt.	FLÅDERBatt 1	>	1300	20	12	34
KAVALERIPRAM	AGGERSHUS	~	1300	20	19	54
BLOKSKIB	DANNEBROG	>	1430	60	53	51
FRIGATE	ELVEN	~	1230	10	9	7
STYKPRAM	HAJEN	>	1445	18	7	6
SOUTHWING			Subtotal	202	139	277
BLOKSKIB	KRONBROG	>	1430	22	18	9
STYKPRAM	SVÆRDFISKEN	>	1430	18	18	19
BLOKSKIB	JYLLAND	>	1430	54	28	43
KAVALERIPRAM	RENDSBORG	>	1500	20	15	35
KAVALERIPRAM	NYBORG	~	1230	20	24	34
BLOKSKIB	WAGRIEN	>	1515	52	21	42
BLOKSKIB	PRØVESTENEN	>	1515	58	40	35
LEGEND ~LEFT >HAULED DOWN FLAG AND PENANT			Subtotal	244	164	217
			Total	**696**	**368**	**640**

ENGLISH UNITS

NORTHWING				
TYPE	NAME	GUNS	DEAD	W'DED
FREGAT	AMAZON	38	14	23
FREGAT	BLANCHE	36	7	9
FREGAT	ALCMENE	32	5	19
FREGAT	ARROW	20	0	0
FREGAT	DART	30	3	1
CENTRE	Subtotal	156	29	52
LINIESKIB	DEFIANCE	74	24	51
LINIESKIB	MONARCH	74	57	163
LINIESKIB	GANGES	74	7	1
LINIESKIB	ELEPHANT	74	10	13
LINIESKIB	GLATTON	54	18	37
SOUTHWING	Subtotal	350	116	264
LINIESKIB	ARDENT	64	30	64
LINIESKIB	EDGAR	74	31	111
LINIESKIB	ISIS	50	33	88
LINIESKIB	POLYPHEMUS	64	6	25
LINIESKIB	BELLONA	74	11	72
LINIESKIB	RUSSELL	74	11	6
FREGAT	DESIREÉ	40		4
KANONBRIGGS	BITER/BOUNCER/FORCE/SPARKLER	4 x 12		
	Subtotal	488	111	370
	Total	**994**	**256**	**686**

BIOGRAPHICAL NOTES

ADMIRAL SIR HYDE PARKER

VICE-ADMIRAL HORATIO NELSON

SIR THOMAS FOLEY

VICE-ADMIRAL WILLIAM BLIGH

SIR WILLIAM STEWART

SIR THOMAS SYDNEY BECKWITH

CAPTAIN JOHANN OLFERT FISCHER

LIEUTENANT PETER WILLEMOES

GUSTAVE DANE

THOMAS ALLEN

Admiral Sir Hyde Parker (1739-1807)

Second son of Sir Hyde Parker (1714-82) he entered the navy, with his father, in the *Vanguard* and was again for two years with his father in the *Cruiser*. In the summer of 1755 he joined the *Medway* with Captain Charles Proby; and, having passed his examination on 7 Nov., 1757, was promoted on 25 Jan., 1758 to be lieutenant of the *Brilliant* with his father whom he followed to the *Norfolk* and *Grafton*. In July 1761 he was appointed by Cornish to the *Lennox*, and on 18 Dec 1762 was promoted to command the *Manila*, from which, on 18 July 1763, he was posted to the *Hussar*, employed during the following years on the North American station under Commodore Hood (afterwards Lord Hood), by whom he was moved, in September 1770, to the Boston. In July 1775 he was appointed to the *Phœnix*, again on the North American station, and in October 1776 was sent by Lord Howe, in command of a small squadron, to occupy the Northern River, by which the enemy was receiving supplies. The passage was blocked by heavy frames forming artificial and iron-pointed snags, on a plan invented by Benjamin Franklin. These were strengthened by sunken vessels and supported by heavily armed gunboats and by guns on shore. The service was ably performed, Parker passing the obstruction though not without loss, capturing two of the gunboats and driving the rest on shore under the batteries. For this important service he was knighted on 21 April 1779.

In July 1778 he was with Howe at New York and off Rhode Island, and afterwards conveyed the troops and co-operated with them in the brilliant little expedition to Savannah in January 1779. The *Phœnix* was then sent home for repairs, and early in 1780 conveyed the trade to Jamaica. On 4 Oct. she was lost on the coast of Cuba in a hurricane. Her men, with few exceptions, were got safely on shore, with provisions, four guns, and ammunition. They entrenched their position and sent a boat to Jamaica for assistance. By the 15th they were all landed in Montego Bay. Returning to England Parker was appointed to the *Latona* frigate, in which he joined his father's flag in the North Sea, and took part in the action on the Doggerbank. In October 1781 he was appointed to the Goliath, one of the fleet under Howe, in the following year, at the relief of Gibraltar, and in the encounter off Cape Spartel. The *Goliath* was afterwards guardship in the Medway, and later France in

1787. Parker was appointed to the *Orion*, which was paid off when the dispute settled. Similarly during the Spanish armament of 1790 he had command of the *Brunswick*, which he resigned in the autumn.

On 1 Feb. 1793 he was promoted to be Rear-Admiral of the White, and was nominated by Lord Hood to be captain of the fleet with him in the Mediterranean. In this capacity he was present at the occupation of Toulon and the reduction of Corsica. On 4 July 1794 he was promoted to the rank of Vice-Admiral, and, on return of Hood to England, hoisted his flag in the *St. George* as third in command under Admiral Hotham, continuing with him during 1795, and taking part in actions of 13 March and 13 July. On his return to England, in the early part of 1796, he was immediately appointed to commander-in-chief at Jamaica. Where, during the next four years, the cruising ships, as stationed by him, were exceptionally fortunate, and brought in a great many prizes – merchantmen, privateers, and ships of war – by which both himself and his country were materially benefited.

He returned home in the end of 1800, and in the following January was appointed commander-in-chief of a fleet destined for the Baltic on account of the threatening attitude of the Northern Confederation, or as it was more commonly known – the Armed Neutrality. As the negotiations with Denmark proved ineffective, and Parker would not consent to adopt the proposal of Lord Nelson, his second in command, and, leaving a sufficient force to overawe Copenhagen, proceed at once to strike a decisive blow against Russia, it was determined to bring the Danes to terms by force. The depth of water before Copenhagen was insufficient for the larger ships, and Parker accepted the offer of Nelson to undertake the service with a detachment of the smaller ships of the line as note herein. Following the victory Parker could not be persuaded to move up the Baltic; he was nervously anxious to secure the communications in his rear, a theoretical necessity which the special circumstances had annulled. A few weeks after the battle he was recalled, Nelson succeeding to the command. Parker had no further service, and died on 16 March 1807. He was twice married; first, to Anne, daughter of John Palmer Boteler, and by her had three sons; secondly, to a daughter of Admiral Sir Richard Onslow.

Vice Admiral Lord Nelson (1758-1805)

Born on the 29th September 1758 at Burnham Thorpe, Norfolk Horatio Nelson was the 6th of 11 children of the Revd. Edmund Nelson, rector of Burnham Thorpe. Nelson's mother was the great niece of Sir Robert Walpole, and the family were linked to the Navy, where patronage was an advantage, as an uncle, Captain Maurice Suckling was a distinguished and influential naval officer (becoming Comptroller of the Navy). Nelson's mother died was he was 9 years of age and this is believed to have had an effect on his personality and his relationship with women. Little is known of his childhood, though he was a daring and determined child, despite being a little physically delicate. He left his Paston School, North Walsham at 13, at his own request, to join his uncle's ship *Raisonnable* as a midshipman on 1st January 1771. In 1771 he transferred to the *Triumph*, a guardship to Nore – was detached to a West Indiaman for sea service and returned to the *Triumph*, where his experience in small craft in the Thames Estuary was invaluable. In 1773 he transferred to the bomb ketch *Carcass* under Captain Lutwidge and during his time on the vessel went to the Arctic where an effort was made to explore the North East passage. Returning he joined the *Seahorse* and saw service in the East Indies as a Midshipman with Troubridge –being rated an Able Seaman in 1774. He was sent home in 1776 due to ill health (malaria) and later in 1776 joined the *Worcester (64*) as acting Lieutenant, thence to the Lowestoft with Captain Locker with whom he retained a friendship for the rest of his life. He passed his examination for Lieutenant in 1777, served in command of a schooner and a brig *Badger*, being promoted Commander in December 1778. Promoted Post Captain before he was 21 he was appointed to the *Hinchinbroke* and in 1780 volunteered to command a naval party supporting the San Juan Expedition. Whilst it was a partial success it resulted in Nelson contracting yellow fever and suffering further ill-health. He returned to Bath and convalescence with Captain Cornwallis in the *Lion*. In August 1781 he was appointed to the *Albemarle (28)* and proceeded on the Baltic Convoy and then to Quebec, and to New York, under Lord Howe and became acquainted with Prince William. In 1783 he was deployed to the West Indies until the end of the war with America. Returning to England, and paying off, the ship's company volunteered to re-engage with him.

Whilst on half pay he toured France in the winter but finally in 1784 he took command of the *Boreas* for the West Indies under Admiral Hughes. His enforcement of the Navigation Laws brought him into disfavour with local interests, which threatened his professional and financial future. During the commission, in March 1785, he met the widow Mrs. Frances Nisbet (son Josiah Nisbet) at Nevis, leading to marriage in 1787. Returning to England a year later he had exceptionally not lost a single man through sickness or accident during the three years of the commission. Laid off on half pay from the *Boreas* he went to Burnham Thorpe with his wife and lived there with his father for the next five years.

In February 1793 he was appointed to the *Agamemnon (64)* his first ship-of-the-line and under Lord Hood was deployed to the Mediterranean during the time Toulon was occupied by the British. Detached to Naples to obtain troops for the garrison he met Sir William and Lady Hamilton and had an audience with King Ferdinand. On route later to occupied Corsica he engaged three frigates and two smaller vessels and in early 1794 he harassed French privateers and supply ships while British troops landed to capture the island. Nelson landed with seamen and cannon in support and was instrumental in the capture of Bastia. Nelson then landed near Calvi where, during an assault on the citadel, rock splinters caused the loss of the sight of his right eye. After a month's siege Calvi surrendered and he received praise for his unremitting zeal and exertion during the engagement. In March 1975 he sailed with 15 sail-of-the-line on the news of 15 French vessels. Nelson, ahead of the fleet, engaged *Ca Ira (80)* struck to Nelson but with the French fleet retreating Admiral Hotham failed to follow up the advantage, saying :- 'We must be content, we have done very well'. Nelson took a contrary view, saying :- 'Now, had we taken 10 sail and had allowed the 11th to escape, when it had been possible to have got at her, I would never have called it well done'. On 1st June he was appointed Colonel of the Chatham Division of Marines. After failing to engage the French fleet off Toulon, Hotham asked to be recalled and was replaced first by Hyde Parker and then Admiral Sir John Jervis. In 1796 Nelson was promoted Commodore and transferred to the *Captain (74*) and seized Elba. Nelson evacuated Corsica in late 1796 and Jervis was ordered to abandon the Mediterranean.

Nelson was then sent in *Minerve* with two frigates from Gibraltar to evacuate Elba, running the gauntlet of a Spanish fleet. The Governor would not leave so Nelson returned to Gibraltar. With Spanish ships threatening, Nelson stopped to pick up a Thomas Masterman Hardy who had launched a jolly-boat in a vain attempt to recover a sailor fallen overboard. He was able to evade the Spanish vessels and join Jervis off Cape St. Vincent. On the 14th February 1797, the battle of Cape St. Vincent took place between 15 British sail-of-the-line and 27 Spanish vessels. During the action Nelson, one of the younger captains in the fleet, now in command of the *Captain*, wore out of the line (to be followed by Collingwood) and cut off the main body of the Spanish fleet. This action was significant resulting in the boarding of the *San Nicholas (80*) and from her onto the *San Josef*, both vessels surrendering to the sudden assault. The victory had an enormous effect on morale at home where Nelson was promoted Rear Admiral and raised to Knight of Bath. His fame spread throughout the country resulting in a number of civic awards.

After the battle of Cape St. Vincent the fleet refitted at Lisbon, Nelson being sent again to Elba, and on his return, in May 1797, transferred his flag to the *Theseus*. In pursuit of reports of Spanish treasure ships in the Canaries Nelson led an abortive attack on Santa Cruz, during which he was shot in the arm and only saved through the intervention of his stepson Josiah Nisbet who fashioned a tourniquet to prevent further loss of blood. The assault incurred unnecessary loss of life and in retrospect was carried out impetuously, the treasure ships having left the port earlier. Invalided he wrote, 'I am become a burden to my friends and useless to my country'. After convalescing at Bath he recovered his health and received acknowledgements in the form of a pension and Freedom of the City of London. In early March 1798 he sailed in the *Vanguard* to rejoin Admiral Jervis (now appointed Lord St. Vincent) at Cadiz. Detached to the Mediterranean with three 74's and five frigates to explore reports of a gathering French fleet he was eventually accorded a further ten sail-of-the-line and sought the enemy who unbeknown had sailed from Toulon for Egypt via Malta. At the outset of the search the *Vanguard* was dismasted in a storm and only survived through the seamanship and courage of Captain Ball in the *Alexander*. The vessels moored off Sardinia to effect repairs and continued the search, without frigates – arriving off Egypt a day ahead of the French who had occupied Malta on route to their major campaign. As the French arrived off the Nile Nelson had sailed north to reprovision, until eventually he received news of the enemy and he returned in great haste to seek a confrontation. During the voyage Nelson discussed with his captains the options for a successful assault on the enemy fleet however they were engaged. Eventually as dusk was falling on the 1st August 1798 the enemy were found moored in Aboukir Bay – 13 sail-of-the-line and four frigates anchored close inshore in their chosen position. Without hesitation Nelson attacked immediately notwithstanding the shoals and the prospect of a night action. With the freedom of action encouraged by their commander some of Nelson's captains sailed inside the enemy and the van was able to be engaged from both sides and was quickly destroyed. During the action *L'Orient* blew up killing Admiral Breuys and by the morning eight had struck, one sunk and one wrecked on the shoals. The French Army were marooned temporarily and failed to make the progress east which they anticipated. Nelson received a head wound during the action, the *Vanguard* being seriously disabled as a result of the action and the earlier storm damage, and limped back to Naples. On arrival at Naples Nelson was hailed as the saviour of Italy and taken care of by Sir William Hamilton, the British Minister, and his wife, Emma. with whom Nelson fell deeply in love. Honours, a peerage included were showered upon him, and he soon involved himself in the affairs of Naples, encouraging the King to act against the French. The advice led to disaster. Ferdinand of Naples was driven from the mainland of Italy and took flight to Sicily under Nelson's protection. It was at Syracuse that the liaison between Nelson and Emma Hamilton developed into a permanent love affair. It was also during this period of his life Nelson, under pressure from the Neapolitan court, committed the one mean and ungenerous action of his life, when on the court's brief return to Naples he was associated in the events leading to the hanging of the republican Commodore Francesco Caracciolo, who had been captured at the surrender of the Neapolitan republican forces. It was shortly after this episode that Nelson, whose presence in Italy could do no further good to his own country, was recalled. He travelled home across Europe by way of Trieste, Vienna, Prague, Dresden, and Hamburg, in company with the Hamiltons, taking four months over the journey and feted everywhere as one of the rare commanders who had enjoyed a decisive success against the all-conquering French.

Back in England, Nelson found his marriage in ruins, the notoriety of his association with Emma Hamilton having preceded his arrival. But he was almost at once re-employed, being appointed second-in-command to Admiral Sir Hyde Parker on an expedition to the Baltic designed to defeat a coalition of northern Powers, the mainspring of which was Paul I. Tsar of Russia.

The Tsar was assassinated and his policy reversed by his successor, Alexander I, but before the momentous news had become known, Nelson, with a detachment of ships of the fleet of comparatively light draught, attacked and defeated the Danish fleet at the hard-fought battle of Copenhagen on 2 April 1801. Returning finally to England he was appointed to command those inshore forces, which were designed to protect the country from invasion, Nelson showed his usual activity in preparing measures of defence, but an attack on the invasion vessels at Boulogne which he planned to take place in August 1801 was repulsed with heavy losses due mainly to the French use of chain anchor cables in place of the more usual hemp. No further opportunity for active service occurred before the brief Peace of Amiens. During the months of this uneasy truce, for it was scarcely more, Nelson lived at Merton, a modest country estate in Surrey which he had acquired and which he shared with Sir William and Lady Hamilton.

Sir William Hamilton died in London on 6 April 1803 and on 16 May, Nelson, now a Vice Admiral of the Blue, was appointed to the command of the Mediterranean Fleet with his flag in *Victory*. For the next two years his duty was to keep close watch on Toulon to prevent the squadron in that port from getting out and joining forces with others from French and Spanish ports. Villeneuve, the French Admiral, twice evaded Nelson's watch. On the first occasion he was driven back to port by stress of weather, but on the second, in April 1805, he got clean away and into the Atlantic before Nelson could be sure of his destination.

Napoleon, by now Emperor of the French, had ordered his Admiral to the West Indies, where he was to take command of a combined fleet which was to assemble from various Mediterranean and Atlantic ports. This was designed to sweep aside the British western squadron, to secure temporary command of the English Channel, and to enable the French Army to cross for an assault on Great Britain.

Nelson, misled partly by false information and partly by the speed of Villeneuve's return when he heard of Nelson's arrival, missed the French fleet, which returned to Europe in haste before the other squadrons from Europe could join. Reaching the Bay of Biscay, Villeneuve's ships fought an inconclusive engagement off Ferrol in July with a squadron under the command of Sir Robert Calder, and eventually took refuge at Cadiz, joining forces with a Spanish squadron there. This combined fleet was blockaded in the port by Collingwood, whose small detachment was soon reinforced. Meanwhile Nelson, on hearing of Villeneuve's departure from the West Indies, followed him back to Europe and then, having satisfied himself that the French fleet had not returned to the Mediterranean, which was still his responsibility, himself sailed for home in the *Victory* for a few days of rest at Merton. He was there when news of Villeneuve's arrival at Cadiz reached England, and he at once posted to the Admiralty to received orders to return to the Mediterranean. He arrived off Cadiz at the end of September 1805 and at once began to plan in meticulous detail for the battle which he knew would come. Villeneuve would have preferred to stay at anchor in Cadiz but Napoleon, his plan of invasion foiled and his army on the march elsewhere, ordered him to take the fleet into the Mediterranean. To make sure that he was obeyed, Napoleon sent another Admiral to take over command of the fleet, a fact of which Villeneuve was aware. The humiliation was too much for him and he ordered his ships to weigh and to make for the Straits of Gibraltar. No move of the enemy ships eluded Nelson's inshore frigates and, within minutes, the news of the combined Franco-Spanish fleet's departure from Cadiz, was on board the flagship. Once he had put to sea, Villeneuve had thoughts of getting back to Cadiz, but in the end he decided to face his great opponent. On 21 October 1805 the last great action of the days of sail was fought out in historic waters off Cape Trafalgar – twenty seven British ships of the line against thirty-three French and Spanish. Nelson won an annihilating victory, but fell in the hour of triumph, struck down by a bullet fired by a marksman in the fighting top of the French *Redoutable*. It was as the British fleet was sailing into action that Nelson gave his signal officer, John Pasco, instructions for hoisting the most famous signal in British naval history.

Nelson was fortunate in his opportunities but had his full share of failure and misfortune. More than once he was lucky not to have been killed in action but his four brilliant successes at Cape St. Vincent, Copenhagen, the

Nile and Trafalgar stamp him as a master tactition, able to infuse his officers and men with his own ardour, and prepared to work to a low factor of safety. His successes were not due to rashness but to a shrewd knowledge of the forces ranged against him. This knowledge, gained in battle, was reinforced by study, for Nelson was not only a keen student of history but was alive to very new tactical development and idea.

He was a supreme example of a leader who could trust his captains, take them fully into his own confidence, and leave them to exercise their own initiative. He received from them not only personal devotion but services in battle which very few other Admirals have inspired.

As a man Nelson was deeply religious and affectionate, and although his marriage foundered as a result of his liaison with Emma Hamilton, this was the sole instance in his life when a long enduring tie was broken through a fault of his own. For a man who died at the age of 47, Nelson left a wealth of letters, memoranda, and dispatches which show his fire, his brilliance, his capacity, his versatility, his loyalty, and generosity to companions in arms, and his kindness to all those (except, in his last years, his wife) who needed it. His flagship at Portsmouth and his tomb in the crypt of St. Paul's Cathedral continue to be places of pilgrimage.

Admiral Sir Thomas Foley (1757-1833)

'Above six feet in height, of a fine presence and figure, with light brown hair, blue eyes of a gentle expression, and a mouth combining firmness with good humour.'

Born in 1757 of a Pembrokeshire family he entered the navy on board the *Otter* in 1770. After serving in her on the Newfoundland station for three years he was in 1774 appointed to the *Antelope*, going out in Jamaica as flagship of Rear-admiral Clark Gayton. While in her he was repeatedly lent to the small craft on the station, and saw a good deal of active cruising against the colonial privateers. He returned to England in the *Antelope* in May 1778; on the 25th was promoted to the rank of lieutenant, and on the 28th was appointed to the America, with Lord Longford. In her, he took part in the operations of the fleet under Keppel in 1778, and Sir Charles Hardy in 1779. In October 1779 he was appointed to the *Prince George* with Rear-Admiral Robert Digby in which he was present at the capture of the Spanish convoy off Cape Finisterre on 8 Jan 1780, the defeat of Langara off Cape St. Vincent on 16 Jan and the subsequent relief of Gibraltar. Continuing in the *Prince George* when she went to North America in 1781, and afterwards to the West Indies with Sir Samuel Hood, Foley was present as a lieutenant in the attempted relief of St. Kitts, in the engagements to the leeward of Dominica on 9 and 12 April 1782. In the following October, on the invaliding of Captain Elphinstone, he was for a few weeks acting captain of the *Warwick* at New York, and on 1 December was confirmed in the rank of commander, and appointed to the *Britannia*, armed ship. In her he continued after the peace and till the beginning of 1785, when be brought her to England and paid her off.

From December 1787 to September 1790 he commanded the *Racehorse* sloop on the home station, and from her was advanced to post rank on 21 Sept. In April 1793 he was appointed to the *St. George* of 98 guns as flag-captain to Rear-Admiral John Gell with whom he went to the Mediterranean, took part in the operations at Toulon and, when Gell was invalided, continuing as flag-captain to Rear-Admiral Sir Hyde Parker (1739-1807) assisted in driving the French squadron into Golfe Jouan (11 June 1794) and in defeating the French fleet in the two engagements off Toulon (13 March, 13 July 1795). In March 1796 he accompanied Parker to the

Britannia, in which he remained with Vice-Admiral Thompson, who relieved Sir Hyde towards the close of the year. As flag-captain to the commander in the second post, Foley thus held an important position in the battle of Cape St. Vincent on St. Valentine's day 1797. He was shortly afterwards appointed to command the *Goliath* of 74 guns, one of the ships sent into the Mediterranean under Captain Troubridge in May 1798 to reinforce Rear-Admiral Sir Horatio Nelson. He thus shared in the operations of the squadron previous to the battle of the Nile, in which he had the distinguished good fortune to lead the English line into action. In doing so he passed round the van of the French line as it lay at anchor, and engaged it on the inside; the ships immediately following did the same, and a part at least of the brilliant and decisive result of the battle has been commonly attributed to this manoeuvre. The *Goliath* continued on the Mediterranean station, attached to the command of Lord Nelson, till towards the close of 1799, when she was sent home.

In the following January, Foley was appointed to the *Elephant* of 74 guns for service in the Channel fleet. In 1801 as noted herein she was sent to the Baltic, continuing attached to fleet until she returned to England in the autumn to be paid off. In September 1805, when Nelson was going out to resume the command of the fleet off Cadiz, he called on Foley and offered him the post of captain of the fleet. Foley's health, however, would not at that time permit him to serve afloat, and was obliged to refuse. On 28 April 1808 he was promoted to the rank of Rear-Admiral, and in 1811 was appointed commander-in-chief in the Downs, in which post he continued till the peace.

On 12 August 1812 he became a Vice-Admiral; was nominated a K.C.B. in January 1815, a G.C.B. on 6 May 1820, and attained the rank of Admiral on 27 May 1825. In May 1830 he was appointed commander-in-chief at Portsmouth, where he died 9 Jan 1833. He was buried in the Garrison Chapel, in a coffin made of some fragments of oak kept from his old ship *Elephant* when she was broken up.

Foley married, in July 1802, Lady Lucy Fitzgerald, and lived for the most part at Abermarlais, Carmarthenshire. He died without issue .

Vice-Admiral William Bligh (1754-1817)

Born in Plymouth in 1754, Bligh served as a navigator and master of the *Resolution* during the last voyage of circumnavigation by Captain James Cook between 1775-9. In 1787 he was appointed by Sir Joseph Banks to command the armed transport *Bounty* to take breadfruit seedlings from Tahiti to the West Indies. Many of his crew formed attachments with Tahitian women and on 28 April 1789, when the ship was off Tofua in the Friendly Islands, a mutiny broke out lead by Fletcher Christian. Bligh was set adrift with eighteen crew in an open launch (just 23 feet long) with 28 gallons of water, 150 pounds of bread, 32 pounds of pork, 6 quarts of rum and 6 bottles of wine. They voyaged 3,600 miles in forty-six days to reach Timor Island, near Java, without charts or other guidance, a tribute to his seamanship. Bligh's alleged behaviour as a cause of the mutiny is disputed but he continued to have difficult relationships throughout his career though never lacking in courage. He played a distinguished part in the battles of Camperdown, and at Copenhagen as noted in this publication. In 1805 Bligh, who had become a Fellow of the Royal Society, was offered the Governorship of New South Wales, a post he assumed in 1806. Bligh was determined to follow his instruction to stamp out the corruption and racketeering then rampant in Sydney. His measures were so successful that in 1808 a mass meeting of Sydney settlers thanked him for his efforts. Bligh had upset those he accused and suspected of corruption. As a result the military, which was involved in the corruption, moved against him placing him under house arrest. He was eventually returned to England: the men who had instituted his arrest and displacement were charged and punished. Promoted Rear-Admiral of the White in 1811 he was appointed Vice-Admiral of the Blue three years later. He died in 1817 and is buried at St. Mary's Church, Lambeth.

Lieutenant-General Sir William Stewart (1774-1827)

Lieutenant-general, born on 10 Jan. 1774, was the second son of John seventh earl of Galloway, by Anne, daughter of Sir James Dashwood, bart. Charles James Stewart was his younger brother. William received a commission as ensign in the 42nd foot on 9 March 1786, became lieutenant in the 67th foot on 14 Oct. 1767, and captain of an independent company on 24 Jan. 1791. In that year he went with Sir Robert Murray Keith to Vienna and to the congress of Sistova. His company was disbanded in December, and he was appointed to the 22nd foot on 31 Oct. 1792. He served with that regiment in the West Indies in 1793-4, and commanded a company in the grenadier battalion at the capture of Martinique and Guadaloupe. He was wounded in the unsuccessful attempt on Point-à-Pitre on 2 July 1794, when Guadaloupe had been recovered by the French. He returned to England in November, and obtained a majority in the 31st foot.

He was made lieutenant-colonel in the army and assistant adjutant-general to Lord Moira's corps on 14 Jan. 1795, and in June he served on the staff of the expedition to Quiberon. On 1 Sept. he was given command of the 67th foot, and went with it to San Domingo. He was commandant at Mole St. Nicholas, with the local rank of colonel, till it was handed over to Toussaint l'Ouverture in August 1798. Returning to Europe, he obtained leave to serve with the Austrian and Russian armies in the campaign of 1799, and was at the battle of Zurich. It was probably what he saw of Croats and Tyrolese in this campaign that led him to propose, in concert with Colonel Coote Manningham, that there should be a corps of riflemen in the British army. The proposal was adopted, and an experimental 'corps of riflemen' was formed in January 1800 by detachments from fourteen regiments. This was brought into the line two years afterwards as the 95th, and eventually became the rifle brigade. Manningham was colonel and Stewart lieutenant-colonel, his commission being dated 25 Aug. 1800. The organisation and training of the corps fell to Stewart, for Manningham was equerry to the king. The standing orders show how much he was in advance of most soldiers of his time. Medals for good conduct and for valour, lectures, school, library, classification in shooting, and athletic exercises were among the means adopted to heighten the efficiency of the corps. He preferred Irish recruits as 'perhaps from being less spoiled

and more hardy than British soldiers, better calculated for light troops.' Charles James Napier was subaltern in the corps in 1802, and wrote of Stewart as open-hearted and honourable in the highest degree, but with much passion, much zeal, and not the least judgement.
In August 1800 Stewart went with three companies of his rifles to Ferrol in Pulteney's expedition, and was dangerously wounded in the first skirmish. He commanded the troops which served as marines in the fleet sent to the Baltic in 1801. He was himself on board Nelson's flagship at Copenhagen, and wrote the best account of the battle. Nelson wrote of him to St. Vincent as 'the rising hope of our army,' and there was a cordial and lasting friendship between them. By Nelson's wish Stewart's first son was named Horatio. Stewart was included in the vote of thanks of parliament, and was made colonel from 2 April.
In 1804 he was appointed brigadier of volunteers in the eastern counties, and in 1805 he published 'Outline of a Plan for the general Reform of the British Land Forces,' in which he recommended for general adoption many of the institutions which he had already introduced into his own corps. In December 1806 he took command of a brigade in Sicily, and three months afterwards went to Egypt with Fraser's expedition. On 3 April he was sent to Rosetta with 2,500 men to avenge Wauchope'' repulse. Though the most ardent soldier, he was afraid of responsibility; he wished that the command had devolved on some one else, and felt 'a sort of inward presentiment that matters would not go well.' In his first reconnaissance he received a bullet-wound in the arm. He invested the town and made batteries, but did not risk an assault. On the 21st the Turks received reinforcements from Cairo, and cut to pieces a detachment of seven hundred men which he had placed at El Hamed, and he had to fight his way back to Alexandria, losing three hundred more on the road.
The expedition returned to Sicily in September, and Stewart was commandant of Syracuse till February 1809, when he came home. He had been promoted major-general on 25 April 1808, and on 31 Aug. 1809 he was made colonel of the 3rd battalion of the corps he had formed, the 95th rifles. He commanded the light brigade in the Walcheren expedition, but was invalided early in September.
In January 1810 he was sent to the Peninsula to command the British and Portuguese troops which were to form part of the garrison of Cadiz. He did well there, but was soon superseded in the chief command by Thomas

Graham. In July he left Cadiz, and was appointed to the 2nd division of Wellington's army under Hill. He was present at Busaco, but could not obtain the medal, as he was not 'personally and particularly engaged.' In December Hill was invalided, and Stewart commanded his corps for a time, but his self-distrust led Wellington to send Beresford to take Hill's place.

In 1811, after Masséna's retreat, the 2nd division – still forming part of Beresford's corps – shared in the first siege of Badajoz, and bore the brunt of the battle of Albuera. The 1st brigade of it (Colborne's) was nearly destroyed there by a sudden attack of French lancers on its rear as it was advancing to charge the French infantry. According to Napier, this happened because 'Stewart, whose boiling courage generally overlaid his judgement, heedlessly led up in column of companies,' without waiting to deploy, as Colborne wished to do. But the charge was made by three deployed battalions (our of four), and, according to Sir Benjamin d'Urban, Beresford's quartermaster-general, Stewart's fault lay rather in rejecting Colborne's proposal to keep a wing of one regiment in column. There can be no doubt that his impetuosity had something to do with the result; but the urgency of the case and the mist which hid the French cavalry go far to excuse him. Beresford had nothing but praise for him in his despatch, and he was thanked by parliament. In July he went home on account of ill-health, and was employed in the eastern district.

In August 1812 he was again appointed to the army in the Peninsula, with the local rank of lieutenant-general. He joined on 6 Dec., and was given command of the 1st division. It comprised the brigade of guards and a question of privilege soon arose, as he was not a guardsman. In April 1813 he was transferred to his old division, the 2nd. On 4 June he became lieutenant-general. At Vittoria he was on the right under Hill, who spoke highly of his conduct. He was included in the thanks of parliament, and was made K.B. on 11 Sept. When Soult tried to relieve Pampeluna, the 2nd division was guarding the passes near Maya, and was attacked on the 25 July by three division of d'Erlon's corps, and forced back. Stewart reached the field late, having been at Elisondo with Hill, and reformed his line. Four Portuguese guns, which were moving by his order to the new position, stuck fast, and were taken by the French. Wellington referred with some asperity to the loss of these guns in a postscript to his despatch. Stewart took part in Hill's action at Buenza on the 30th, and the next day he led the attack on the French rearguard at the Dona Maria pass. In this attack he was badly wounded, having been already slightly wounded on the 25th. He was present at the Nivelle, Nive, and Orthes, and had a prominent part in the combat of Aire and a minor part at Toulouse. He was popular with the men of his division, among whom he was know as 'auld grog Willie' on account of the extra allowances of rum which he authorised, and which Wellington made him pay for. For his services in the Peninsula he received the gold cross with two clasps, the Portuguese order of the Tower and Sword, and the Spanish order of San Fernando. On 2 Jan 1815 he received the G.C.B.

Stewart had been M.P. for Saltash in 1795, and for Wigtonshire from 1796 onward, and on 24 June 1814 the speaker thanked him in his place, on behalf of the house, for his share in the victories of Vittoria and Orthes, and in the intermediate operations. He saw no further service. His health was broken by seventeen campaigns, in which he had received six wounds and four contusions, and in 1816 he resigned his seat in parliament. In July 1818 he was transferred to the colonelcy of the 1st battalion of what had then become the rifle brigade. He settled at Cumloden on the borders of Wigton and Kirkcudbrightshire, near the family seat. He died there on 7 Jan. 1827, and was buried at Minigaff. In 1804 he had married Frances, daughter of the Hon. John Douglas, and he left one son, Horatio, a captain in the rifle brigade and one daughter, Louisa.

Sir Thomas Sydney Beckwith (1772-1831)

With Craufurd shares the honour of being one of the finest leaders of light troops ever known, was the third son of Major-general John Beckwith, who commanded the 20th regiment at Minden, and four of whose sons became distinguished general officers. He was appointed lieutenant in the 71st regiment in 1791, and at once proceeded to join it in India. He found Lieutenant-colonel Baird in command of the regiment, and under him learned both how to lead and how to organise a regiment. With the 71st he was present at the siege of Seringapatam in 1792, at the capture of Pondicherry by Colonel Baird in 1793, and during the operations in Ceylon in 1795. He was promoted captain in 1794, and returned to England with the head-quarters of his regiment in 1798. He had established his reputation as a good officer in India, and when in 1800 he volunteered for a company in Manningham's new rifle corps his services were accepted. Colonel Manningham had proposed to the Horse Guards to be allowed to raise a regiment of light troops to be specially organised for outpost duties, after the manner of the French voltigeurs. His offer was accepted, and volunteers were called for from every regiment. Beckwith had in the 71st made the acquaintance of William Stewart, the lieutenant-colonel of the new rifle corps, and obtained a captaincy under his friend. He soon got his company into such good order that it was ordered to accompany the expedition to Copenhagen in 1801, where it's adjutant was killed. He was promoted major in Manningham's rifles, now called the 95th, in 1802, and formed one of the officers whom Sir John Moore trained at Shorncliffe. He became lieutenant-colonel in 1803, and under Moore's supervision got his regiment into model order. He was admired by his officers and adored by his men, whose health and amusement were always his first consideration. In 1806 he served in Lord Cathcart's abortive expedition to Hanover, and in 1807 his regiment formed part of the division which, under their future commander, then Sir Arthur Wellesley, won the battle of Kioge in Denmark, when it was thanked in the general's despatch. In July 1808 he accompanied General Acland to Portugal, and was present at the battle of Vimeiro. After the arrival of Sir John Moore, and on his taking the command of the troops in Portugal, the 95th was brigaded with the 43rd and the 52nd under the command of General Anstruther, and formed part of the reserve under General Paget.

The conduct of this brigade, and more especially of the 95th regiment under Beckwith, has been described by Napier; it closed the retreat, and was daily engaged with the French, but though suffering the most terrible privations it never broke line, or in any way relaxed its discipline. The regiment particularly distinguished itself at Cacabelcos, where it faced round and with the help of the 10th Hussars fought successfully the whole advanced guard of the French army. The 95th and Beckwith crowned their service at Corunna, when they were the last troops to leave the city, and managed to take with them 7 French officers and 156 men, whom they had made prisoners on the previous day. In 1809 the 95th was again brigaded with the 43rd and the 52nd, and sent to the Peninsula. Craufurd was leading them up to the main army, when he heard that a great battle had been fought, and that General Wellesley was killed. Nothing daunted he pressed forward and after a forced march of twenty-five hours reached Talavera on the evening of the battle. When Lord Wellington retired from Spain and cantoned his army on the Coa, the light brigade was stationed far in front to watch the French movements. In their advanced position there were frequent conflicts, all described by Napier, in which the 95th and Beckwith proved their efficiency. At the skirmish of Barba del Puerco and the battle of Busaco the light brigade won the especial praise of Lord Wellington, and when in 1811 it was increased by three Portuguese regiments to a division, Beckwith received the command of one of the brigades. The division led the pursuit of Massena, was warmly engaged at Pombal, Redinha, and Foz d'Aronce, and defeated a whole *corps d'armee*, though with great loss, at Sabugal. In this engagement Beckwith particularly distinguished himself, was wounded in the forehead, and had his horse shot under him. The perfect discipline and valour of his men were again proved, and the disgraceful blunders of Sir William Erskine (1769-1813) who had temporarily succeeded Craufurd, were remedied by the men's gallantry. Shortly after the battle of Fuentes d'Onor Beckwith was obliged to return to England from ill-health, and to hand over his perfect regiment and brigade to Colonel Barnard. He had inspired his men with such confidence 'that they would follow him through fire and water when the day of trial came' (COPE, *History of the Rifle Brigade*, p.53). On his health being restored he was knight in 1812, as proxy for his brother George, made a knight of the Tower and Sword of Portugal in 1813, and in 1812 appointed assistant quartermaster-general in Canada. In that capacity he commanded an expedition to the coast of the

United States, which took Littlehampton and Ocrakoke, and had Charles Napier under him as brigadier. In 1814 he was promoted major-general, and was (1815) among the first K.C.B's. He saw no more active service, but in 1827 was made colonel commandant of his old corps, and rifle brigade, which he had done so much to organise. In 1829 he was appointed commander-in-chief at Bombay, in 1830 he became lieutenant-general, and on 15 January 1831 died at Mahableshwur of fever. The light division was the greatest creation of Sir John Moore; its services appear in every page of the history of the Peninsular war, and Sidney Beckwith was the practical creator of one of the most distinguished regiments. 'He was', according to Kincaid, 'one of the ablest outpost generals, and few officers knew so well how to make the most of a small force'.

Captain Johann Olfert Fischer (1747-1829)

Fischer's family were originally Dutch. His father had become a Vice Admiral in the Danish Navy and had married twice having 14 children by his second wife. The eldest of these was Johann Olfert. He was a skilful naval captain and had commanded a frigate, Bornholme, on the West Indies station in the years 1784-1789. It is believed he met Nelson visiting the Danish Virgin Islands in 1786 and 1787.

In January 1801 Fischer was a senior captain and 'commander of the defences of Copenhagen Roads' – a stretch of sea forming the approaches to the city. Fischer was hampered by the command structure as he was not the most senior officer in the Danish navy. The Admiralty included Admiral Kaas and Vice Admiral Wleugal who were already members of the Defence Commission when Fischer joined it on 1st January 1801. Nor was Fischer the only captain charged with the defence of Copenhagen. Steen Bille was in charge of a separate squadron of ships covering the actual approach to the harbour. Bille and Fischer could not give orders to each other even though their two squadrons would form an inverted V only 600 yards apart at their nearest point. Finally, decision making was not left to the Navy. The Crown Prince of Denmark was involved in and made all decisions. He acted as Commander in Chief. It would have been much more sensible if the Crown Prince had appointed a Commander in Chief of the Navy (say Kaas) with Fischer reporting into Kaas and responsible for the whole defence. As it was the Crown Prince would sometimes ignore the more senior naval officers and issue orders to Bille and Fischer. Another worrying sign was that the Defence Commission (apart from ensuring normal fitting out of warships as Spring approached) made no preparations for offence or defence until 20th February.

Then there was the issue of the quality of the ships and men Fischer was to have as his command. Fischer's forces consisted of old cut down three deckers, cavalry carriers and floating batteries. His own flagship the Dannebroge of 60 guns had a single stump mast. With all the ships and batteries moored, some to four anchors and the rest to two, this was going to be very much a defensive battle with no possibility of the attack being

taken to the attackers unless Bille's squadron could be used to accomplish this and the absence of a single command would prevent this from happening.
Then there was the question of the quality of the men. Fischer wrote "most of the defence ships have only two sea officers and the crews are poorly exercised and on the last ship sent out (Elven) hardly exercised at all. I am only praying for good weather so that I can moor them up and get the ships properly manned and exercised."
In the short time that was available, by working day and night Fischer was able to construct a defensive line which was going to put up a stiff resistance to Nelson's attack. However he made two errors either of which if they had not been made would have rendered Nelson's task much more difficult, if not impossible.
The first was the actual positioning of his defensive line. It was actually poorly positioned to defend the city against an attack from either North or South. Only two of his ships could open fire on a force steering for the harbour channel. To the South the British bomb vessels could have destroyed the arsenal after Nelson took out only three of Fischer's ships. More serious was the fact that there was sufficient deep water for Nelson to attack both sides of the Danish ships repeating his strategy at the battle of the Nile. Fortunately for the Danes Nelson did not discover this. All of this could have been countered if Fischer had anchored his ships in parallel ie. across the channels not vertically. Why he and the Danish high command did not think of doing so has never been satisfactorily explained.
The second error was Fischer's reaction to Nelson's surveying of the approaches. He made no attempt to send out frigates to drive off the Amazon and sink the ships when they anchored as markers. He did not send out boats to cut the buoys adrift in the darkness and attack the surveying parties. When faced with an opponent of Nelson's capability this was complacency indeed.
Nevertheless when action began at 10.30 in the morning there was much to be proud of: the Danish gunnery, the tenacity of the men serving the guns and the firepower of the floating batteries. As Fischer wrote to the Crown Prince: "At half past eleven the Dannebroge was set on fire. I repaired with my flag on board the Holsteen but the Dannebroge long kept her flag flying in spite of this disaster". There was no doubting Fischer's bravery.

He crossed to his next ship the Holsteen in an open boat. When resistance was shown to be fruitless he then went to the Trekoner fort. He had been wounded in the head during the battle.

Bravery however was not enough. The faulty command structure prevented Bille's division, which had sails, from automatically coming to Fischer's aid. Bille did not offer and Fischer did not ask. By 2pm out of 19 Danish ships only 4 were still in action. At 5pm Fischer ordered the guns to stop firing.

Accepting the mistakes that had been made the Danes had fought as best they could. Fischer however then committed a blunder which perhaps shows his lack of confidence in his ability. Fine though the performance of his ships had been, in his report he misrepresented the battle and claimed that some of the actions of Nelson's ships had not been in accordance with accepted standards. He claimed two British ships had surrendered and then rehoisted their colours. He also cast doubts on the reasons behind Nelson's truce. This was unnecessary and ungenerous. Nelson was furious and replied to Fischer's report. The Danish Chief Minister was inclined to take a reasonable viewpoint. Lindholm wrote to Nelson "I do not conceive that Commodore Fischer had the least idea of claiming as victory, what to every intent and purpose was a defeat. He has only thought that this defeat was not an inglorious one, and that our officers and men displayed much bravery and firmness against forces so superior in every respect".

Brave, methodical and hard working, Fischer was simply beaten by his own limitations and outclassed by his opponent. He survived to be Vice Admiral and died in 1829.

Lieutenant Peter Willemoes (1783-1808)

Denmark is a land made up of many islands and her people are therefore natural sailors. Great sailors she had, though many of their names are hardly known to English people. Peter Willemoes who is the subject of this article, had a short if brilliant career, he did not reach higher in rank than that of lieutenant, and he died before the age of 25.

He made for himself a place in the history of the Danish Navy and in the hearts of the Danish people; a hero, much likened to young Nelson. In Denmark everyone takes Peter Willemoes for granted; he is a national possession. In their navy, ships have been named after him, his name appears on streets and at the theatre; a play, and Grundvig's memorial poem do him honour. In his native town of Assens he is best remembered of all the local celebrities.

If you ask a Dane about Willemoes he will undoubtedly bring to mind Lord Nelson, and this should awaken our interest at once. In all the books which portray Nelson at Copenhagen, we find little of any mention of Willemoes; if mention there is it is meagre and inaccurate.

Peter's grandparents descended from country folk in Jutland, somewhere north of the Liim Fiord. This borders closely on reclaimed peat-land known as Store Vildmose, and we may assume there is a connection with 'Vildmose' (Wild Moss) and the origin of the family name. It is interesting to note that in this part of Jutland the Danish spoken is so like the English of our own East Anglia.

Christian Willemoes, Peter's father, was manager of the Wedellsborg estate of the Island of Fyn, from 1768 to 1780. In 1780 he was promoted to Receiver of Revenues for the two western counties of the Island, and he made his headquarters at Assens. Here, at Willemoesgaarden, on the 11th May 1783 Peter Willemoes was born, being the fifth child of his parents. Peter went to school on his native island of Fyn, the school being situated on the estate of County Johan Ludvig Reventlow. In the autumn of 1795, being 12 years of age, Peter entered upon his 5 year course as a Naval Cadet; the Academy being one of the four stately buildings making up the fine square of Amalienborg Plads. Very little is known of Willemoe's Academy time, he appears to have been a popular and lively young man, somewhat sensitive for his calling. His yearly reports, still preserved in Copenhagen, are much like most school reports; good enough but not remarkable, his conduct being "Fairly good". One of his best subjects, however, was Gunnery, and he also studied English language.

On 29th August, 1800, Peter was promoted to Sekond Lieutenant, being just 17 years old, and was appointed to the third-rate *Prindsesse Louise Angusta*, 64, Captain Hans Schultz. On March 1st, 1800, he was attached to a new 74, the *Dannemark*, Captain Steen Bille. This officer was also a native of Assens and it is quite possible that there was a keen interest shown in the young Willemoes, which may have been a contributing factor in his appointment to the command of his celebrated Gerner's *Floating Battery No. 1.*
Floating Battery No. 1 was built in 1786 by Henrick Gerner, Chief of Naval Construction at the Copenhagen Navy-Yard. It's dimensions were: Length 140 ft.Width 41 ft. Draught 3 ft. 3 ins. She carried 24 brass 24 pounders (12 each side) and was the only craft of its kind in the Danish Line. It was a raft on which one had to work ankle-deep in water; it had a flimsy looking breastwork in place of bulwarks, no masts, rigging or rudder, and was propelled with oars and/or some species of warp. It was so low in the water that most of the shots fired from a Ship-of-the-Line passed over it; it was the nearest thing to a submarine in that era, and had the capacity to get 'between wind and water' (a shot below the water-line). The English Squadron, anchored in Kings Deep, compared with fighting under sail, would not be rolling very much and therefore less likely to expose vital parts to the 'wind and water' water-line area to the low level guns such as Willemoes commanded.
Willemoes was positioned in the Danish Line between the *Dannebrog* and the *Sjælland* and during the early stages of the battle the British ships took little notice of him. Once all the ships had taken station, the battle became one long artillery duel, and as Nelson said "Here was no manoeuvring; it was downright fighting". Therefore the little *Floating Battery No.1* did not receive much attention until the *Elephant* became aware that she was receiving fire of a very damaging nature. The marine sharp-shooters on board the *Elephant* were ordered to fire at Willemoe's Battery, but proving ineffective, the gun-deck gave the Battery it's attention, although the Dane's low profile acted as a safeguard.

Willemoes now found that he did not only have the *Elephant* from which he was receiving shot, but also two other men-of-war to contend with, (most likely the *Glatton*, astern of Nelson, and/or the *Ganges* and the *Monarch* ahead). Willemoes was being fired at with ball, grape and dismantling shot (he afterwards wrote of this to his family) and in this situation he continued to fight his Battery for some three hours. He finally had to cut his cables, owing to the Danish Commodore's ship, *Dannebrog*, being in flames and becoming a menace to her own line as to warrant an immediate decision as to their best course of action. Willemoes therefore cut his four anchors loose, drifting as the stream carried them northward.

The Battery drifted on and ran foul of the bows of the *Sjælland*, next astern. Together, being unable to get clear, the 74 also cut her cables and drifted down almost to Trekroner. Willemoes was able to free his Battery, but came for a short while under the fire of Parker's Squadron. He managed to warp his way into the safety of the shoal called 'Stubben', where he spent the night and wrote his report to the Danish Admiralty.

Willemoes had carried his fight against all the might of the Line-of-Battleships, and had continued to fire his guns long after the majority of his own Line had been silenced. All through the battle the young officer had been full of enthusiasm and had encouraged his men at their guns. The Battery had undergone considerable damage and it was a miracle that he had come out alive. Peter had fought until almost 40% of his crew were either killed or wounded (128 being his complement on that day) many of which were transferred to the *Sjælland.* Much damage had been done to No. 1 Battery. Five gun carriages totally destroyed, many others damaged; one gun burst, another damaged, the breastwork on both sides destroyed, and the casemate damaged by shot. Willemoes's ensign had twice been shot away, and when finally lost, he had to resort to the use of a dead marine's red coat.

All this had been observed by Nelson throughout the length of the battle, and he had been amazed to see a "mere boy" in command of this somewhat unusual fighting machine. He was much taken with the young man's devotion to his duty, and the gallant fight he had observed with admiration from the *Elephant.* Nelson had said as much to Colonel Stewart, although Stewart did not, on this occasion, quote his exact words. Colonel

Stewart tells us (in his private journal) that: "No. 14 continued his fire longer and actually did the Elephant more damage than the Line-of-Battleships"(*Dannebrog*).

After his share in the 'Day of Honour', Peter Willemoes is well remembered for his presentation to Nelson, at Nelson's request, at the Palace of the Crown Prince some six days after the battle. History has recorded that Nelson told the Crown Prince that Willemoes should be an Admiral. Willemoes was the ideal of much of the populace and a sword of Honour was duly presented to him by the ladies of Kiel (a Danish city in those days) and parents christened their children Peter, Petrea and Willemoesina.

Surprisingly, Peter Willemoes was not promoted to a full lieutenant until over six years later. In the following March of 1808, not yet 25 years of age, he was killed on board the Ship-of-the-Line *Prins Chrisian Frederik*, in an epic action against a superior force of two British Ships-of-the-Line. This battle took place at Sjælland Odde, and north-western tip of Zealand. He was buried with others from the battle in the little churchyard of Odden, close to where the fight took place.

At Willemoesgaardens Museum, Assens, there are rooms in which keepsakes of this young hero are displayed, including paintings and a model of Floating Battery No. 1. Also in the town today, the Willemoes statue is to be found, produced by a Danish sculptor by the name of Peters, also a native Fyn. The simple inscription reads: "Peter Willemoes, 1783-1808". Peter stands, 'for ever young and for ever watchful', looking, as he must himself have looked, across the narrow strip of Kings Deep, (towards Nelson's gigantic *Elephant*), his hand resting on his dirk; his right hand holding the linstock with which he touched off his brass 24-pounders. He was a boy, but I prefer to think that he stood like a man.'

Gustave Dane (1776-1856)

Listed on the *Elephant* Muster as Gustave Dani, subsequently anglicised as a George Dani, he was born in 1776 in Pisa, Tuscany. He left home at the early age of 11 to go on board a British man-of-war and remained in the service until 1806. He served under Sir John Jervis and Lord Nelson, and was present at the battles of St. Vincent, the Nile and Copenhagen. (Hilda Gamlin (Nelson's Friendships Vol II by Hutchinson & Co 1899)) recorded that Dani was present at the rudderhead as Nelson sealed the invitation to a truce.)

He was afterwards engaged in the service of the City of Dublin Steam Packet Company, and was for upwards of 25 years their respected servant, only retiring three years before his death in 1856. He received a gold medal for meritorious aid to those on board the burning ship *Ocean Monarch*, off the Great Ormes Head in August 1848, and also for his previous naval engagements.

George Dani died on November 28th 1856 at his residence 30 Brunel Street, Liverpool. (His residence, like Nelson's, no longer stands.) He was interred in St James Cemetery, Liverpool, in a grave already occupied by his wife, Mary Anne, who died ten years before him. His death certificate states that he was 80 years old and that the cause of death was 'disease of the heart, 3 years certified', it also tells us that his occupation was 'Master Mariner'. The informant is given as G. Dani, presumably his son who lived at 2 North Street, Toxteth Park, Liverpool. Dani's headstone incorrectly gives his age as 75 years. It has been moved from its original site and has become somewhat damaged. St James Cemetery, like so many others, has been rearranged by the local council in order to make it easier to maintain. Many gravestones have been damaged and some lost for ever, but along with Dani, we have found five more of Nelsons Heroes mentioned elsewhere in this publication (Nelson's Heroes).

The obituary of George Dani appeared in the *Liverpool Daily Post*, Tuesday 2nd December 1856, and reads:-

'On the 28th November 1856, at his residence Brunel St., Everton, Captain George Dani. Deeply regretted. He fought with Nelson at the battles of the Nile, Copenhagen and St. Vincent. He was also for many years in the service of the City of Dublin Steam Packet Company.

It is stated earlier that Dani had received a gold medal for giving aid to the passengers and crew of the burning ship *Ocean Monarch* and the following extract from the *Liverpool Mercury* for August 29th 1848 shows the brave seaman acting as one would expect;

The following is a correct statement from Captain G. Daney (this surname is spelt incorrectly) of the City of Dublin Steamer '*Prince of Wales*' who, seeing the distressed situation of the Ocean Monarch while on his passage from his port to Beaumaris, in the most praiseworthy manner, bore down towards her and was happily the means of saving the lives of a large number of passengers. After the gallant captain and crew had rendered all assistance in their power and had seen the last people taken from the wreck, the steamer, having some of the people on board who were saved by their humane exertions, proceeded to her destination where she arrived at 8 o'clock. Captain Daney' s statement:- "When outside the lightship I discovered a ship on fire, bearing about 12 miles N.W. I immediately hauled up for her and ordered one of the boats to be got ready, in going along I discovered a boat with four hands in it. I took her in tow and in a short time after I saw a man floating on a part of the wreck. I sent a boat to pick him up and got him on board. At this time there was a great deal of the wreck floating about. I lowered my boat and sent Mr. Batty, the mate, and three hands to see if they could pick up anyone alive. As Mr. Batty was going into the boat, he discovered the body of a child not quite dead, but it was too far gone to recover. I then proceeded to the ship on fire and got three more passengers that were floating. When I came up to the ship she was in one flame from fore to aft. I did not think it prudent to go alongside of her but I came to anchor close ahead of her. At this time the wind was increasing and a heavy sea running, and so much of the wreck hanging about the vessel the boats could not approach her in safety. I then got the passengers to assist me to weigh anchor and returned to pick up my own boat. I then returned to the ship and saw from twenty to thirty people under the bowsprit of the ship. I then came to anchor close on her starboard bow and got lines attached to the boats and saved everyone that was left on the wreck. At this trying moment Mr. Batty was of the greatest service to me as well as all other hands who cheerfully and willingly assisted me in saving all they could."

Vice Admiral Lord Nelson.

Pastel by Johann Heinrich Schmidt 1800

Picture courtesy of
National Maritime Museum, London

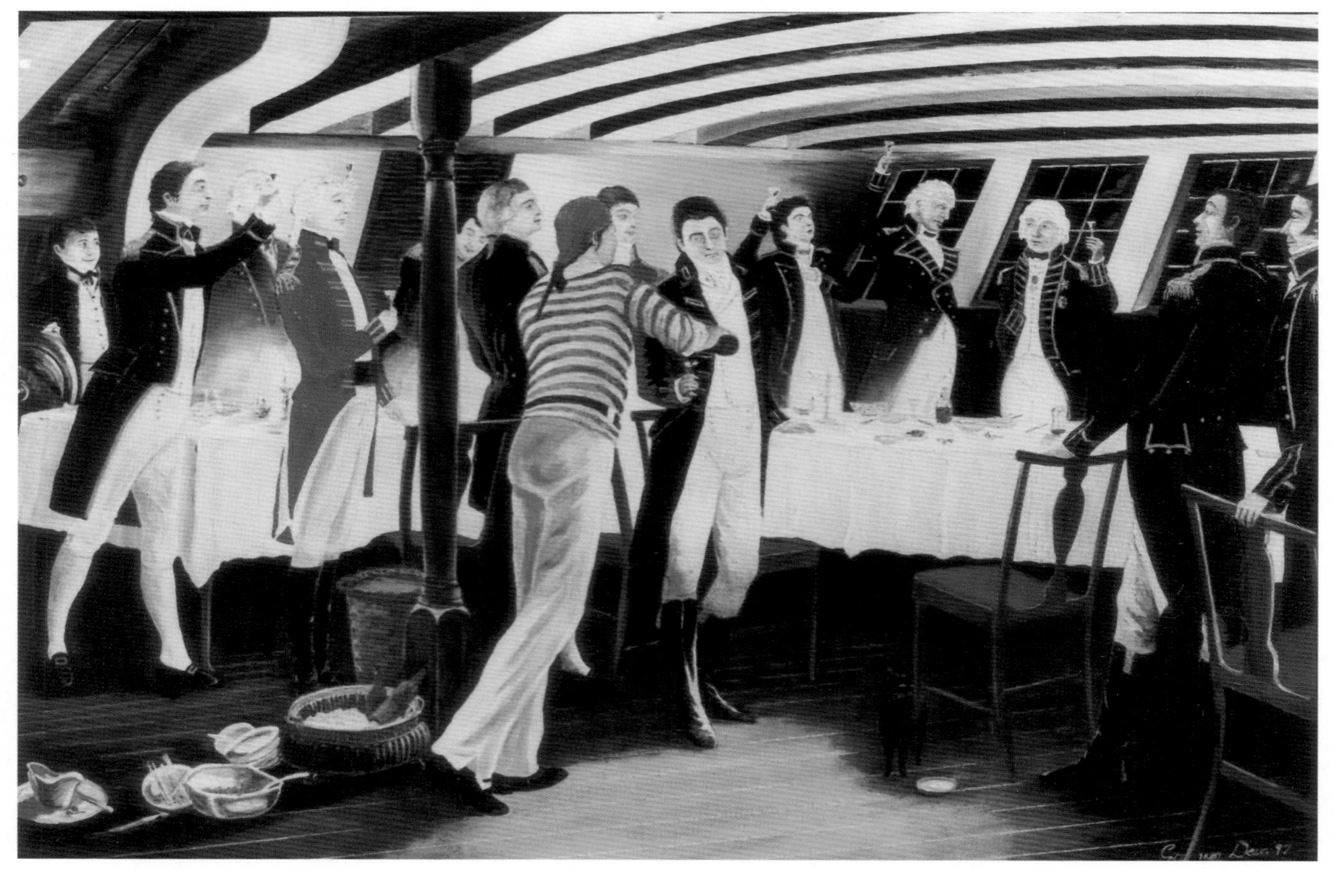

HARDY-COL. STEWART-FOLEY-RIOU-INMAN-ADML. GRAVES-NELSON-FREMANTLE

"Evening before Copenhagen" by Graham Dean after Thomas Davidson Courtesy: Tony Dickinson

Nelson's *Elephant* at the battle of Copenhagen. By S.Francis Smitheman ATD BA(Hons) F.R.S.A., in co-operation with The Royal Naval Museum, Portsmouth.

THE DEFEAT of the DANISH FLEET and BATTERIES off COPENHAGEN, THE 2ND OF APRIL 1801
Engraving by PW Tomkins after the painting by JT Serres (1759-1825) son of Dominic Serres (1725-1893)
With kind permission of Warwick Leadlay Gallery

No 16 was Nelson's favourite signal - it indicated 'close action'. He always informed his captains that when in doubt they would do no harm to lay their ship alongside that of the enemy.

No 39 was the famous signal used at Copenhagen by Admiral Sir Hyde Parker 'Break off action'. Nelson chose to ignore it and went on to win the battle.

Flag Illustration
No 16
Close Action

Flag Illustration
No 39
Break off Action

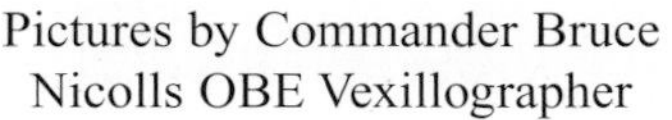

Pictures by Commander Bruce Nicolls OBE Vexillographer

 The Bronze Gilt Davidson Nile Medal, presented to Colonel Stewart by Nelson after the Battle. The riband is blue and loop suspension for the medal is unusual - The Sim Comfort Collection.

Admiral Sir Hyde Parker

by James Roberts 1781 National Maritime Museum.

Illustration of *Elephanten* figurehead and stern. Royal Danish Naval Museum, Copenhagen.

Thomas Allen (1771-1838)

Thomas Allen was born in the village of Sculthorpe, near Burnham Thorpe, Norfolk, in the year 1771. From the earliest years, Thomas was in the service of the Nelson family, and when Horatio took command of the *Agamemnon* (64), Tom Allen, with others from the area went along with the young captain to start his career in the Royal Navy. On board the *Agamemnon*, Tom was rated as Nelson's servant and accompanied him at all times. During the action he would be stationed at one of the upper deck guns close to his master; on more than one occasion, when under fire, he interposed his bulky form to shield the much smaller Nelson. It is said that once, during a desperate boat action, he actually placed his own head between Nelson and an attacker and received a severe wound in doing so.

Tom Allen was in charge of Nelson's personal effects, his jewels, plate, valuables, and all things belonging to him on board. He also acted as body servant, and as such, he often had to coax his little master from a wet deck and a raging storm. It has been said that he was too familiar with Nelson: on one occasion he told him off, in front of other officers, for taking an extra glass of wine, by saying, "no more now, you know it will only make you ill".

Tom was for some time at Nelson's home, Merton Place, but he did not go with the hero to Trafalgar; who knows, if he had, perhaps Nelson would have survived the battle. After Nelson's death, Tom returned to Burnham Thorpe, but without a pension of any sort he soon became very poor. He was saved from the workhouse only by the intervention of Sir Thomas Hardy, who was then governor of Greenwich Hospital. Hardy appointed him pewterer to the Hospital, and it was from this comfortable situation he was called by a very sudden death. He is buried in the old cemetery Greenwich, close to the grave of Captain Hardy. There is a fine memorial to him still standing above his grave and the inscription is as follows:- '*To the Memory of Thomas Allen The Faithful Servant of Admiral Lord Nelson Born at Burnham Thorpe in the County of Norfolk 1764 and died at the Royal Hospital Greenwich on the 23rd November 1838.*

MUSTER LIST

HMS ELEPHANT

For genealogists and historians alike, muster lists provide a useful source of information in respect of those who served as part of a ship's company. Samuel Pepys, who had a thirst for knowledge, would have appreciated the sight of students poring over Muster Books at the Public Record Office. As Secretary to the Admiralty he set in progress improvements to the professionalism of the Navy, and would have recognised and endorsed the structured process which required ship's officers to complete a weekly muster of the ship's complement. Entitlement to e.g. bounty, victualling, required proof, and the captain, purser, master and boatswain endorsed each two monthly summary enabling those who follow to verify the names of those who served their sovereign on the high seas. The following are amongst the matters listed on the muster: - Bounty Paid – Individual Number - Date and year of entry on ship - Appearance on board - When and whether pressed or not - Place and county where born (seamen only – Marines and Officers did not suffer the indignity of submitting their personal details, presumably on the basis that they were unlikely to abscond, and have to be subsequently chased) - Number and letter of tickets (in the case of men transferred to another ship) – Man's name – Qualities.

Youths under 15yrs rated Boys 3rd Class (BBB1), under 18yrs, 2nd Class (BB1) and;
those training as officers Boys 1st Class (B1)

Adults with no experience = Landsman Useful but not expert or skilful = Ordinary Seaman
Able and well acquainted = Able Seaman
Warrant Officer ranks = Boatswain Gunner Boatswains Mate Quarter Gunner

The details summarised in the following pages are interpreted from the written record (ADM 36/15342) at the Public Record Office, Kew.

MUSTER TABLE

(ADM 36/15342)

The Muster Table was the leading page, indicating where each weekly muster had been held. The table used in this publication covers the eight week period 1st March to 30th April 1801., commencing therefore at the time when the ship was at Portsmouth under the control of the Clerk of Check and ending when the vessel was in the Baltic Sea after the battle of Copenhagen. The entries for the second week show that the ship was in 'Yarmouth Roads'; on the third week 'At Sea'; the fourth in 'Copenhagen Roads', where she remained for three weeks; being shown in the 'Baltic Sea'.for the final two weeks.

The summary shows a complement of 595 mustered in groupings of:-

	Wk1	Wk2	Wk3	Wk4	**Wk5**	Wk6	Wk7	Wk8
Ship's Company	430	429	429	429	**423**	418	417	416
Volunteers and Boys	22	22	28	28	**28**	29	29	29
Marines Part of Complement	111	111	111	111	**108**	107	107	107
Supernumeraries for Wages.	39	33	29	182	**5**	33	43	43
Prisoners at 2/3 allowance	4	4	4	4	**29**	3	3	3

Week five records losses from the *Elephant* muster list in the battle of Copenhagen. Required to be signed by four officers this muster is signed by Captain Thomas Foley, Master George Andrews, Purser Joseph Jones and Boatswain Hugh Mitchell, and is handsomely written in a broad copper-plate hand.

The Muster shows that following the battle, between 1st May and 30th June, the *Elephant* was 'At Sea' 6th May – 'At Revel' 14th May, continuing 'At Sea' till arriving 'Kioge Bay' on 26th June and 'Dantzig Bay' 30th June.

Surname	First	Qualities	No.	Age	Born	Entered	Appeared	Previous
ABDOLA	Hamel	LM	354	20	Constantinople	01/07/1800	01/07/1800	Former Books
ADAMS	John	PteRM	33			01/07/1800	01/07/1800	Former Books
AGAR	John	Ord.	350	32	Ireland	01/07/1800	01/07/1800	Former Books
AINSLY	Thomas	AB	364	29	Carlisle	01/07/1800	01/07/1800	Former Books
ALICK	John	LM	427	20	Sweden	01/07/1800	01/07/1800	Former Books
ALLEN(2)	John	LM	520	20	Saugham	20/06/1800	10/10/1800	SL No.103
ALSOP	John	Yeoman Sheets	155	34	Southwark	01/07/1800	01/07/1800	Former Books
ALVES	Basil	1st Lieut RM	27			01/07/1800	01/07/1800	Former Books
ANDERSON	James	AB	89	23	Pathead	01/07/1800	01/07/1800	Former Books
ANDREWS	George	Master	13			01/07/1800	01/07/1800	Former Books
ANNEY	John	AB	271	20	Plymouth	01/07/1800	01/07/1800	Former Books

Discharged dead 2nd April 1801 slain in fight with the enemy

Surname	First	Qualities	No.	Age	Born	Entered	Appeared	Previous
ANTONIO	Carlo	Boy	BBB2	13	Naples	01/07/1800	01/07/1800	Former books
APPLEBY	John	AB	104	32	Shields	01/07/1800	01/07/1800	Former Books
		Quarter Gunner 01/09/1800						
ARMOUR	David	Ord.	88	34	Greenock	01/07/1800	01/07/1800	Former Books
ARNOLOR	Peter	Pte.RM	82			01/07/1800	01/07/1800	Former Books
ASHTON	Thomas	AB	250	23	Liverpool	01/07/1800	01/07/1800	Former Books
ATHA	Anthony	LM	178	29	London	01/07/1800	01/07/1800	Former Books
AURNES	John	Ord.	426	22	Hamburgh	01/07/1800	01/07/1800	Former Books
AUSTIN	Saml.	Sgt RM	29			01/07/1800	01/07/1800	Former Books
AXX	William	Quarter Master	172	35	Greenwich	01/07/1800	01/07/1800	Former Books
BAAD	Willm. M	LM	467	20	At Sea	01/07/1800	01/07/1800	Former Books
Lent to Danish prize 27 Jan 1801								

Surname	First	Qualities	No.	Age	Born	Entered	Appeared	Previous
BAILEY	Stephen	Ord.	412	23	Limerick	01/07/1800	01/07/1800	Former Books
BAILEY	Thomas	Pte.RM	38			01/07/1800	01/07/1800	Former Books
BAKER	John	AB	372	39	Wisbeach	01/07/1800	01/07/1800	Former Books
Discharged dead 21st April 1801 fell over board and was drowned								
BAKER	Joseph	Pte.RM	74			01/07/1800	01/07/1800	Former Books
BARNES	George	Pte.RM	81			01/07/1800	01/07/1800	Former Books
BARNES	Joseph	Pte.RM	122			26/12/1800	26/12/1800	Plymouth HQ
BARRETT	William	Steward	323	26	Plymouth	01/07/1800	01/07/1800	Former Books
BARRY	David	LM	345	26	Ireland	01/07/1800	01/07/1800	Former Books
BARRON	John	Ord.	84	23	Northumberlnd	01/07/1800	01/07/1800	Former Books
BARRY	George A	Mid.	145	17	London	01/07/1800	01/07/1800	Former Books
		Master's Mate 2nd April 01						

Surname	First	Qualities	No.	Age Born	Entered	Appeared	Previous
BAZEY Discharged dead 02/04/01 Slain in fight	Henry	Quarter Gunner	120	51 Funnell Argyleshire	01/07/1800	01/07/1800	Former Books
BEAUMONT	Geo.	Drummer	32	Royal Marines	01/07/1800	01/07/1800	Former Books
BECKETT	Thos.	LM	505	20 Bolton	06/07/1800	29/07/1800	Beaulieu HS
BEDFORD	Willm.	Yeoman Sheets	473	40 Cullompton	01/07/1800	01/07/1800	Former Books
BELL	James	Ord.	93	41 Hexham	01/07/1800	01/07/1800	Former Books
BELL	John	Ord.	423	23 Malta	01/07/1800	01/07/1800	Former Books
BELRINGER	John	LM	501	30 Dorset	27/07/1800	27/07/1800	Ethalion
BEVANS	William	Pte.RM	117		26/12/1800	26/12/1800	Plymouth HQ
BEVERAGE	John	Ord.	65	26 Pathead	01/07/1800	01/07/1800	Former Books
BLAKE	Chis.	Ord.	428	22 Dublin	01/07/1800	01/07/1800	Former Books

Surname	First	Qualities	No.	Age	Born	Entered	Appeared	Previous
BOND	Anthy.	Ord.	142	37	Gibraltar	01/07/1800	01/07/1800	Former Books
BOND	Peter	Ord.	325	29	London	01/07/1800	01/07/1800	Former Books
BONIFANTI	Bartw.	LM	480	18	Ajaccio	01/07/1800	01/07/1800	Former books
BOLTON	Thomas	AB	368	25	Sunderland	01/07/1800	01/07/1800	Former Books
		Quarter Gunner 01/09/1800						
Discharged dead 7th April 1801 of wounds received in fight on 2nd inst.								
BORNELL	Anthy.	Ord.	73	24	Lincoln	01/07/1800	01/07/1800	Former Books
BOURN	William	Sailmkrs	166	34	Aberdeen	01/07/1800	01/07/1800	Former Books
Power of attorney 27/02/00 Mate								
BOWETH	Thomas	Mid.	147	30	Alnwich	01/07/1800	01/07/1800	Former Books
Lent 27 Jany. 1801 to a Danish Prize								
BOYDE	John	Ord.	411	32	Isle of Man	01/07/1800	01/07/1800	Former Books
BRADFIELD	John	Ord.	285	26	Norfolk	01/07/1800	01/07/1800	Former Books

Surname	First	Qualities	No.	Age	Born	Entered	Appeared	Previous
BRADLEY	John	Pte.RM Corporal 01/11/1800	35			01/07/1800	01/07/1800	Former Books
BRAGG	James	AB	374	22	Chichester	01/07/1800	01/07/1800	Former Books
BRANTON	Wm.	Carpntrs Crew	47	27	Hull	01/07/1800	01/07/1800	Former Books
BRICHELL	Stephen	Ord.	316	22	Somerset	01/07/1800	01/07/1800	Former Books
BRIGHTON	James	Ord.	522	20	Rochdale	31/05/1800	10/10/1800	SL No.106
BRINIGER	John C	AB Ord 01/11/1800	136	32	Hanover	01/07/1800	01/07/1800	Former Books
BROPHY	John	CorpRM	3			01/07/1800	01/07/1800	Former Books
BROWN	Benj.	Pte.RM	72			01/07/1800	01/07/1800	Former Books
BROWN	John	Ord.	57	30	London	01/07/1800	01/07/1800	Former Books
BROWN(3)	John	Ord. AB 01/09/1800	523	25	Dublin	31/05/1800	31/05/1800	SL No. 107

Surname	First	Qualities	No.	Age	Born	Entered	Appeared	Previous
BROWN	Thomas	Lieut	12			01/07/1800	01/07/1800	Former Books
Discharged 06/04/1801 invalided								
BROWSIN	Willm.	Armr's	486	32	London	01/07/1800	01/07/1800	Former Books
BRYANT	John	AB Ord. 01/11/1800	397	29	Tipperary	01/07/1800	01/07/1800	Former Books
BRYANT	John	Pte RM	19			01/07/1800	01/07/1800	Former Books
BUCHANAN	Geo.	AB	387	40	Kembleton	01/07/1800	01/07/1800	Former Books
BUCHANAN	John	AB	382	30	Sterlingshire North Britain	01/07/1800	01/07/1800	Former Books
BUCHANAN	Robert	LM	351	27	London	01/07/1800	01/07/1800	Former Books
BUCKINGHAM	John	Carpntrs Crew	92	55	Lowestofte	01/07/1800	01/07/1800	Former Books
BURCH	Peter	Mid.	137	29	Plymth Dock	01/07/1800	01/07/1800	Former Books
Discharged 9th April 1801 on promotion to Holstien pay list								

Surname	First	Qualities	No.	Age	Born	Entered	Appeared	Previous
BURGEFS	John	Boatswns Mate	177	30	Deptford	01/07/1800	01/07/1800	Former Books
Discharged 09/04/01 Holstien on promotion								
BURNE(1)	Edw.	LM	221	32	Dublin	01/07/1800	01/07/1800	Former Books
BURNE(2)	Edwd.	LM	454	31	Wicklow	01/07/1800	01/07/1800	Former Books
BUSCOTT	Edwd.	Ord.	220	21	Jersey	01/07/1800	01/07/1800	Former Books
BUSHNAN	James	Quarter Masters Mate	483	37	Stretford	01/07/1800	01/07/1800	Former Books
BUSKIN	John	Ord.	494	20	Somerset	03/07/1800	01/07/1800	Beaulieu Chatham HS
BUTLER	John	AB Ord 01/11/1800	394	40	Kilkenny	01/07/1800	01/07/1800	Former Books
BYLES	William	Ord.	70	24	Suffolk	01/07/1800	01/07/1800	Former Books
CALL	Richd.	AB	44	30	Borton	01/07/1800	01/07/1800	Former Books
CANNON	John	LM	196	30	Ireland	01/07/1800	01/07/1800	Former Books

Surname	First	Qualities	No.	Age	Born	Entered	Appeared	Previous
CANNON	John	Pte RM	23			01/07/1800	01/07/1800	Former Books
CARDWICH	Henry	Ord.	298	25	Northampton	01/07/1800	01/07/1800	Former Books
CARPENTER	Wm.	Ord.	291	24	London	01/07/1800	01/07/1800	Former Books
CARROLL	Chris.	AB Ord 01/11/1800	404	31	Drogerty	01/07/1800	01/07/1800	Former Books
CARSON	Thomas	Ord.	126	24	Ontaff	01/07/1800	01/07/1800	Former Books
CAVILL	Willm.	Pte.RM	97			01/07/1800	01/07/1800	Former Books
CHALMERS	James	LM	61	21	Pathead	01/07/1800	01/07/1800	Former Books
CHALMERS	Robert	Ord.	68	26	Pathead	01/07/1800	01/07/1800	Former Books
CHAMBERS	John	Ord.	27	27	Rochester	01/07/1800	01/07/1800	Former Books
CHIVERS	James	Pte.RM	91			01/07/1800	01/07/1800	Former Books
CLAPPERTON	Jno.	1st Lieut.	132		Royal Marines	26/12/1800	26/12/1800	Plymouth HQ

Surname	First	Qualities	No.	Age	Born	Entered	Appeared	Previous
CLARK	Danl.	AB Ord 01/04/1801	389	50	Cork	01/07/1800	01/07/1800	Former Books
CLEARY	Michl.	Ord.	293	27	Cork	01/07/1800	01/07/1800	Former Books
COADY	Willm.	Quarter	521	26	Dublin	01/07/1800	10/10/1800	SL No.104
COLE	John	LM	186	25	Middlesex	01/07/1800	01/07/1800	Former Books
COLE	Robert	AB	408	20	Bristol	01/07/1800	01/07/1800	Former Books
COLEMAN	Robert	AB	269	31	Millbrook Port Somerset	01/07/1800	01/07/1800	Former Books
COLEMAN	Willm.	Pte.RM	124			26/12/1800	26/12/1800	Plymouth HQ
COLLINS	James	Pte.RM	89			01/07/1800	01/07/1800	Former Books
COLLINS	Thos.	AB	530	36	Waterford	03/01/1800	09/03/1800	R.William
COLLINS	William	Ord.	86	20	Deal	01/07/1800	01/07/1800	Former Books
COLLONEN	John	AB	268	20	Cork	01/07/1800	01/07/1800	Former Books

Surname	First	Qualities	No.	Age	Born	Entered	Appeared	Previous
COLLONWAY	Chris.	AB	242	25	New York	01/07/1800	01/07/1800	Former Books
CONGEWILLL	James	Carpntrs Crew	124	30	London	01/07/1800	01/07/1800	Former Books
CONNELL	Danl.	LM	202	24	London	01/07/1800	01/07/1800	Former Books
CONSULLY	Pedro	Pte.RM	36			01/07/1800	01/07/1800	Former Books
CONTEUR	Anthy.	Pte.RM	83			01/07/1800	01/07/1800	Former Books
COOK	James	Pte.RM	109			20/09/1800	20/09/1800	Plymouth HQ
COOK	Robert	Pte.RM	118			26/12/1800	26/12/1800	Plymouth HQ
COOKES	James	LM	510	21	Tipperary	11/07/1800	29/07/1800	Beaulieu HS
Power of attorney 1st Jany 1801 to father								
COOKES	Joseph	Ord.	410	30	Manchester	01/07/1800	01/07/1800	Former Books
COOMBS	Lawce.	Pte.RM	126			26/12/1800	26/12/1800	Plymouth HQ

Surname	First	Qualities	No.	Age Born	Entered	Appeared	Previous
COOPER	Thos.	Pte.RM	78		01/07/1800	01/07/1800	Former Books
Discharged dead 2nd April 1801 slain in fight							
COX	Edward	Pte.RM	10		01/07/1800	01/07/1800	Former Books
COX	John	Pte.RM	44		01/07/1800	01/07/1800	Former Books
COX	John	Boy	BB21	13 Portsey	01/03/1801	13/03/1801	Vol.Portsmouth
CRABTREE	John	Ord.	329	23 Lancashire	01/07/1800	01/07/1800	Former Books
CRAMP	Joseph	Pte.RM	96		01/07/1800	01/07/1800	Former Books
CRAWFORD	John	AB	252	30 Glasgow	01/07/1800	01/07/1800	Former Books
CRENCHE	James	Pte.RM	47		01/07/1800	01/07/1800	Former Books
CRENTHER	John	Pte.RM	57		01/07/1800	01/07/1800	Former Books
CRICHTON	Robt	Surgeon	236	Warrant	01/07/1800	01/07/1800	Former Books
CROFS	George	Pte.RM	52		01/07/1800	01/07/1800	Former books

Surname	First	Qualities	No.	Age	Born	Entered	Appeared	Previous
CUMPENNY	Richd.	AB	58	29	Hearne Kent	01/07/1800	01/07/1800	Former Books
CUMMINGS	James	Quarter Gunner	353	55	Newcastle	01/07/1800	01/07/1800	Former Books
CUMMINGS	John	AB	83	36	Durham	01/07/1800	01/07/1800	Former Books
CUMMINGS	Joseph	AB	265	26	Waterford	01/07/1800	01/07/1800	Former Books
CUNNINGHAM	Michl.	Ord.	425	22	Dublin	01/07/1800	01/07/1800	Former Books
CURDY	John	Ord.	253	31	Bristol	01/07/1800	01/07/1800	Former books
CURLING	Robert	Ord.	21	42	Chatham	01/07/1800	01/07/1800	Former Books
Discharged Dead 27/04/1801 on board								
DAMON	Geo.	AB Ord. 01/11/1800	477	22	Pool	01/07/1800	01/07/1800	Former Books
DANE*	Gustave	Ord. (Trumpeter)	226	22	Leghorn	01/07/1800	01/07/1800	Former Books

Surname	First	Qualities	No.	Age	Born	Entered	Appeared	Previous
DARWOOD	Geo.	Quarter Master	168	20	Fifeshire	01/07/1800	01/07/1800	Former Books
DAVENPORT	Thos.	Pte.RM	68			01/07/1800	01/07/1800	Former Books
DAVIDSON	John	LM	453	22	Stepney	01/07/1800	01/07/1800	Former Books
DAVIE	John	AB	362	26	Falmouth	01/07/1800	01/07/1800	Former Books
DAVIES	Charles	Volunteer	B11	13	Salisbury	10/03/1801	10/03/1801	Vol.Portsmouth
DAVIES	Danl.	Pte.RM	100			24/07/1800	24/07/1800	Plymouth HQ
DAVIES	John	Sailmkrs Crew	100	30	Bristol	01/07/1800	01/07/1800	Former Books
DAVIES	Joseph	Chaplain	343	By warrant		01/07/1800	01/07/1800	Former Books
DAVIES	Robt.	AB	373	34	Holywell	01/07/1800	01/07/1800	Former Books
DAWSON	Thomas	AB	471	20	Lancashire	01/07/1800	01/07/1800	Former Books
DAWSON	Willm.	Ord.	302	20	Edingburgh	01/07/1800	01/07/1800	Former Books

Surname	First	Qualities	No.	Age	Born	Entered	Appeared	Previous
DAY	Thomas	AB	474	24	London	01/07/1800	01/07/1800	Former Books
DEANS	James	AB	114	37	Huntingdon	01/07/1800	01/07/1800	Former Books
DEANS	William	AB Ord. 1/11/1800	479	57	Greenwich	01/07/1800	01/07/1800	Former Books
DELANEY	Timy.	Quarter Gunner	149	24	Kilkenny	01/07/1800	01/07/1800	Former Books
DEMPSEY	Willm.	AB	369	29	Queens Co.	01/07/1800	01/07/1800	Former Books
DIGBY	Richd.	AB	407	39	Dublin	01/07/1800	01/07/1800	Former Books
DIOS	Robt.	LM	460	20	Ireland	01/07/1800	01/07/1800	Former Books
DOAKULL	Henry	Cooks Mate	26	30	Bafsonbury	01/07/1800	01/07/1800	Former Books
DOWNING	Michl.	AB	535	26	Ireland	03/01/1800	09/03/1800	R.William
DOYLE	Thomas	LM	490	35	Waterford	01/07/1800	01/07/1800	Former Books

Surname	First	Qualities	No.	Age	Born	Entered	Appeared	Previous
DREDGE	Wm.	Pte.RM	42			01/07/1800	01/07/1800	Former Books
DRIVER	James	Boy	BBB15	15	Plymouth	01/07/1800	01/07/1800	Former books
DUCKERWELL	Hm.B	Ord.	417	22	Oxford	01/07/1800	01/07/1800	Former Books
DUDLEY	William	AB	35	43	Lynn	01/07/1800	01/07/1800	Former Books
DUN	Peter	Qrtr Gnr	538	30	Ireland	07/01/1801	09/03/1801	HS P. Charlotte
DUNCAN	William	Ord. AB 01/11/1800	331	21	S.Shields	01/07/1800	01/07/1800	Former Books
DUNN	Michl.	AB Ord 01/11/1800	400	29	Cork	01/07/1800	01/07/1800	Former Books
DUNN	Thomas	Ord.	289	29	Ireland	01/07/1800	01/07/1800	Former Books
DURIN	Geovani	Carpntrs	134	30	Trieste Italy	01/07/1800	01/07/1800	Former Books
DYER	George E	Coxswns Mate	225	40	Braywick	01/07/1800	01/07/1800	Former Books

Surname	First	Qualities	No.	Age	Born	Entered	Appeared	Previous
EASON	John	Pte.RM	65			01/07/1800	01/07/1800	Former Books
EASTMORE	Charles	AB	537	32	N.Yarmouth	11/12/1800	11/12/1800	R.Wm Malta
		Quarter Master's Mate 02/04/1801						
EDWARDS	Thomas	AB	23	25	London	01/07/1800	01/07/1800	Former Books
ELKINS	John	Pte.RM	73			01/07/1800	01/07/1800	Former Books
Discharged dead 2nd April 1801 slain in fight								
ELLIS(1)	Edward	AB	36	22	Horton, Yorks	01/07/1800	01/07/1800	Former Books
ELLIS(2)	Edward	AB	399	35	Cornwall	01/07/1800	01/07/1800	Former Books
ENSTEY	Charles	AB	254	39	Leith	01/07/1800	01/07/1800	Former Books
EVANS	Davd.	LM	500	19	Exeter	19/07/1800	19/07/1800	Ethalion
EVANS	Evan	LM	56	20	London	01/07/1800	01/07/1800	Former Books
EVANS	Henry	Pte.RM	110			26/12/1800	26/12/1800	Plymouth HQ
EVANS	Herbert	Boy	BB15	12	Haverfordwest	18/12/1800	13/03/1801	Vol. Holden

Surname	First	Qualities	No.	Age	Born	Entered	Appeared	Previous
EVANS	James	Boy	BBB9	14	London	01/07/1800	01/07/1800	Former Books
EVANS	Richd.	AB	266	36	Devon	01/07/1800	01/07/1800	Former Books
EVANS(2)	Richd.	Ord.	327	26	America	01/07/1800	01/07/1800	Former Books
EVELEIGH	John	Ord.	496	27	Waterford	05/07/1800	05/07/1800	Volunteer
FANCY	Robert	AB Ord 1/11/1800	476	23	Hudland	01/07/1800	01/07/1800	Former Books
FARRELL	Robert	Ord.	69	25	Pathead	01/07/1800	01/07/1800	Former Books
FARRELL	Thomas	LM	442	21	Cork	01/07/1800	01/07/1800	Former Books
FARRELL	Wm.	LM	434	22	Ireland	01/07/1800	01/07/1800	Former Books
FAY	Thomas	AB Ord. 01/11/1800	392	41	Chichester	01/07/1800	01/07/1800	Former Books
FERGUSON*	John	Ord.	66	23	Pathead	01/07/1800	01/07/1800	Former Books
FERNADREWS	Peter	Ord.	421	26	Portugal	01/07/1800	01/07/1800	Former Books

Surname	First	Qualities	No.	Age	Born	Entered	Appeared	Previous
FITCHETT	Thos.	Corp.RM		94		01/07/1800	01/07/1800	Former Books
FITZGERALD	John	LM	198	30	Ireland	01/07/1800	01/07/1800	Former Books
FITZPATRICK	Bry.	AB	270	26	America	01/07/1800	01/07/1800	Former Books
FLANNERY	Patk.	LM	195	30	Ireland	01/07/1800	01/07/1800	Former Books
FLEMMING	Timy.	AB 01/11/1800 Ord.	388	30	Tiperrary	01/07/1800	01/07/1800	Former Books
FLINN	James	AB	492	23	Dorset	06/06/1800	01/07/1800	Beaulieu Chatham HS
FOLEY	Richard	Mid.	489	14	Haverfordwest	01/07/1800	01/07/1800	Former Books
FOLEY	Thomas	Captain	14			01/07/1800	01/07/1800	Former Books
FOOT	John	LM	182	45	Somerset	01/07/1800	01/07/1800	Former Books
FOOTMAN	William	LM	378	35	London	01/07/1800	01/07/1800	Former Books
FOWLE	William	Pte.RM	112			26/12/1800	26/12/1800	Plymouth HQ

Surname	First	Qualities	No.	Age	Born	Entered	Appeared	Previous
FOWLER	Nathl.	Pte.RM	85			01/07/1800	01/07/1800	Former Books
FOX	Charles	Ord.	34	31	Leicester	01/07/1800	01/07/1800	Former Books
FOX	Henry	AB	384	30	At sea	01/07/1800	01/07/1800	Former Books
FRANCES	Arnolai?	Boy	BB20	13	Haverfordwest	01/03/1801	13/03/1801	Vol. Holden
FRANKS	Robt.	LM	222	26	London	01/07/1800	01/07/1800	Former Books
Will 10th June 1800								
FREEMAN	Willm.	Ord.	220	24	London	01/07/1800	01/07/1800	Former Books
FRENCH	Joseph	Pte.RM	53			01/07/1800	01/07/1800	Former Books
Discharged 13/04/1801 sent sick Holstien Hospital Ship								
FRISKA	Youhan	LM	210	40	Germany	01/07/1800	01/07/1800	Former Books
FRYER	Henry	Mid.	139	29	Greenwich	01/07/1800	01/07/1800	Former Books
Discharged 9th April 1801 Holstien pay list on promotion								
FRYER	Harrison	Mid.	487	14	Wells	01/07/1800	01/07/1800	Former Books

Surname	First	Qualities	No.	Age	Born	Entered	Appeared	Previous
FRYER	William	LM	443	23	London	01/07/1800	01/07/1800	Former Books
FULLER	William	AB	348	24	Canterbury	01/07/1800	01/07/1800	Former Books
GALLON	James 01/10/1800	Corporal Quarter Masters Mate	241	36	Northumber-land	01/07/1800	01/07/1800	Former Books
GARRICK	David	AB	110	20	Dublin	01/07/1800	01/07/1800	Former Books
GEORGE	Robert	LM	440	19	Gilford	01/07/1800	01/07/1800	Former Books
GIBBS	John	Pte.	99	Royal Marines		01/07/1800	01/07/1800	Former Books
GIBBS	Richd.	Surgeons 2nd Mate	528			05/02/1800	05/02/1800	Viper cutter
GILBERT	Joseph	AB	55	26	Bedford	01/07/1800	01/07/1800	Former Books
GILLIMAN	Frans.	Pte.RM	5			01/07/1800	01/07/1800	Former Books
GIFSARD	Thos.	LM	504	21	Hansbury	04/07/1800	29/07/1800	Beaulieu HS
GILLARD	John	Pte.RM	129			26/12/1800	26/12/1800	Plymouth HQ

Surname	First	Qualities	No.	Age	Born	Entered	Appeared	Previous
GOODLING	John	Ord.	91	26	London	01/07/1800	01/07/1800	Former Books
GOOCH	Henry	AB	273	27	N.Yarmouth	01/07/1800	01/07/1800	Former Books
		Quarter Gunner 01/09/1800						
GORTON	John	Boy	BBB10	13	London	01/07/1800	01/07/1800	Former Books
GREEK	John	Boy	BBB4	13	Malta	01/07/1800	01/07/1800	Former Books
GREEK	Phillip	Pte.RM	71			01/07/1800	01/07/1800	Former Books
GREEN	Owen	Pte.RM	95			01/07/1800	01/07/1800	Former Books
GREEN	Thomas	LM	190	32	Gloucester	01/07/1800	01/07/1800	Former Books
GROWERS	John	LM	464	19	Clerkenwell	01/07/1800	01/07/1800	Former Books
GUTTRIDGE	Thos.	LM	436	19	Nottingham	01/07/1800	01/07/1800	Former Books
HALFORD	Giles	Boy	BBB12	13	London	01/07/1800	01/07/1800	Former Books
HALL	Joseph	AB	98	42	Alston Moor	01/07/1800	01/07/1800	Former Books

Surname	First	Qualities	No.	Age	Born	Entered	Appeared	Previous
HALL	Willm.	Pte.RM	62			01/07/1800	01/07/1800	Former Books
HALLERAN	Peter	Ord.	377	32	Co.Clair	01/07/1800	01/07/1800	Former Books
HAMILTON	Benj.	Pte.RM	60			01/07/1800	01/07/1800	Former Books
HAMMON(2)	John	AB	396	30	Rosecommon Ireland	01/07/1800	01/07/1800	Former Books
HAMMOND*	Phillip	LM	439	22	Jersey	01/07/1800	01/07/1800	Former Books
HANNON	John	Quarter Gunner	51	27	Whitby	01/07/1800	01/07/1800	Former Books
HARDCASTLE	Willm.	Ord. AB 01/04/1801	76	24	Nottingham	01/07/1800	01/07/1800	Former Books
HARDING	Saml.	Pte.RM	98			01/07/1800	01/07/1800	Former Books
HARLAND	John	Ord.	318	23	Wexford	01/07/1800	01/07/1800	Former Books
HARNETT	James	Pte.RM	76			01/07/1800	01/07/1800	Former Books

Surname	First	Qualities	No.	Age	Born	Entered	Appeared	Previous
HARRIS	James	LM	194	33	London	01/07/1800	01/07/1800	Former Books
HARTON	William	Carpntrs Crew	157	24	Yorkshire	01/07/1800	01/07/1800	Former Books
HAWKINS	Abram.	Ord.	46	30	London	01/07/1800	01/07/1800	Former Books
HELLING	John	LM	183	50	Lancashire	01/07/1800	01/07/1800	Former Books
HENDERSON	James	Ord.	20	32	Newcastle	01/07/1800	01/07/1800	Former Books
HENDLEY	Richd.	AB	249	37	Dublin	01/07/1800	01/07/1800	Former Books
HENDLEY	William	AB 01/11/1800 Ord.	356	37	Charlton	01/07/1800	01/07/1800	Former Books
HIGGINS	James	Mid.	513	17	Nevis WI	01/08/1800	01/08/1800	1st Class Boys
HIGGINS	Robt.	Corporal	174	31	Tyrone	01/07/1800	01/07/1800	Former Books
HIGGINS	Thos.	LM	429	29	Wicklow	01/07/1800	01/07/1800	Former Books

Surname	First	Qualities	No.	Age	Born	Entered	Appeared	Previous
HILL	Frans.	AB	361	36	London	01/07/1800	01/07/1800	Former Books
Will & power atty. 12/05/1800			Quarter Gunner 01/09/1800					
HILL	Isaac	Ord.	292	23	Westminster	01/07/1800	01/07/1800	Former Books
HILL	John	AB	122	36	London	01/07/1800	01/07/1800	Former Books
HILL*	John	Boy	BB1	14	London	01/07/1800	01/07/1800	Former Books
HITCHINS	Seaman?	LM	502	19	Lancashire	01/07/1800	29/07/1800	Beaulieu HS
HOGG	Robert	Cooper	115	44	London	01/07/1800	01/07/1800	Former Books
HOLK	Holk	LM	509	20	Denby Wales	02/07/1800	29/07/1800	Beaulieu HS
Sick 13/04/1801 Holstein HS								
HOLMES	Willm.	LM	499	20	Exeter	19/07/1800	19/07/1800	Ethalion
HOLSTON	John	AB	390	26	Windsor	01/07/1800	01/07/1800	Former Books
		Ord. 01/11/1800						
HOLSTON	William	AB	103	26	Norway	01/07/1800	01/07/1800	Former Books

Surname	First	Qualities	No.	Age	Born	Entered	Appeared	Previous
HOMEWARD	William	AB	30	24	Cobham	01/07/1800	01/07/1800	Former Books
HONEYBALL	Edwd.	LM	203	20	London	01/07/1800	01/07/1800	Former Books
HOOLE	Willm.	LM	506	19	Manchester	08/07/1800	29/07/1800	Beaulieu HS
HORAM	William	Ord.	300	23	Dublin	01/07/1800	01/07/1800	Former Books
HOUNSON	Richd.	Pte RM	17			01/07/1800	01/07/1800	Former Books
HOWELL	William	AB	514	20	Haverfordwest	02/08/1800	02/08/1800	Vol. Chapman
		Ord 02/10/1800 Trumpeter 11/03/1801						
HOY	John	Boatswn Mate	178	47	Virginia	01/07/1800	01/07/1800	Former Books
Will and Power 24 Feb 1800 to wife								
HUGHES	Griffith	AB	533	22	N. Wales	03/01/1800	09/03/1800	R.William
HUNTER	Joseph	LM	466	34	Co. Derry	01/07/1800	01/07/1800	Former Books
HURZE	William	LM	354	22	Wilton Wilts	01/07/1800	01/07/1800	Former Books

Surname	First	Qualities	No.	Age	Born	Entered	Appeared	Previous
HUSBAND	Robt.	Quarter Master	165	33	Whitby	01/07/1800	01/07/1800	Former Books
ILES	William	Pte.RM	34			01/07/1800	01/07/1800	Former Books
IMBERLY	Joseph	Ord.	303	20	Plymouth	01/07/1800	01/07/1800	Former Books
INGLESBY	Robt.	Ord.	409	24	London	01/07/1800	01/07/1800	Former Books
INNES	James	LM	452	23	Liverpool	01/07/1800	01/07/1800	Former Books
Discharged dead 2nd April 1801 slain in fight with the enemy								
JAMES	George	AB	151	29	S. Wales	01/07/1800	01/07/1800	Former Books
JAMES	Morgan	Boy	BB16	12	Cardigan	16/01/1800	13/03/1801	V. Holden
JAMES	William	Lieut.	15			01/07/1800	01/07/1800	Former Books
JAMESON	John	LM	438	23	Scotland	01/07/1800	01/07/1800	Former Books
JERVIS	John	Sgt RM	30			01/07/1800	01/07/1800	Former Books
JOHNSON*	John	AB	272	29	N.Yarmouth	01/07/1800	01/07/1800	Former Books

Surname	First	Qualities	No.	Age	Born	Entered	Appeared	Previous
JOHNSON	William	AB	17	37	Jamaica	01/07/1800	01/07/1800	Former Books
JOHNSON	Wm.	Vol.	B13	14	Kircaldie	10/03/1801	10/03/1801	2nd Class Boys
JOINT	Rich.	AB	267	20	Devon	01/07/1800	01/07/1800	Former Books
Will and Power 25th May 1800								
JONES	Jacob	Boy	B15	15	Haverfordwest	15/12/1800	13/03/1801	Vol.Holden
JONES	John	Ord.	326	21	London	01/07/1800	01/07/1800	Former Books
JONES	John	Pte.RM	93			01/07/1800	01/07/1800	Former Books
JONES	Joseph	Purser	478	By warrant		01/07/1800	01/07/1800	Former Books
JONES	Roger	Pte.RM	7			01/07/1800	01/07/1800	Former Books
JONES	Thomas	Pte.RM	50			01/07/1800	01/07/1800	Former Books
JORDAIN	George	Ord.	109	20	London	01/07/1800	01/07/1800	Former Books
JORDAIN	John	AB	532	40	Baltimore	03/01/1800	09/03/1800	R. William

Surname	First	Qualities	No.	Age	Born	Entered	Appeared	Previous
JOYCE	Thomas	Qrtr Mstr	152	35	New York	01/07/1800	01/07/1800	Former Books
JUSTICE	James	LM	380	55	Fifeshire	01/07/1800	01/07/1800	Former Books
KEARNES	Paul	AB Ord. 01/11/1800	391	30	Dublin	01/07/1800	01/07/1800	Former Books
KELLY	Hugh	Ord.	413	40	Dublin	01/07/1800	01/07/1800	Former Books
KELLY	John	LM	197	23	Sufsex	01/07/1800	01/07/1800	Former Books
KELLY	Thomas	AB Ord. 01/11/1800	385	47	Dublin	01/07/1800	01/07/1800	Former Books
KELLYAN	Jermh.	Boy	BBB8	14	London	01/07/1800	01/07/1800	Former Books
KENNYMORE	Thos.	Ord.	128	20	Galway	01/07/1800	01/07/1800	Former Books
KINGROVE	Alex.	Ord.	305	22	Chatham	01/07/1800	01/07/1800	Former Books
KINNEAR	George	Ord.	284	46	Swansea	01/07/1800	01/07/1800	Former Books

Surname	First	Qualities	No.	Age	Born	Entered	Appeared	Previous
KIPPING	Robt.	QMster	138	32	Yarmouth	01/07/1800	01/07/1800	Former Books
Discharged 9th April 1801 on promotion to Holstien pay list								
KYLE*	George	Mid.	524	20	Donegal	17/10/1800	17/10/1800	Vol. Chapman
		19/11/1800 Master's Mate						
LANDGRIDGE	John	Pte.RM	58			01/07/1800	01/07/1800	Former Books
LANEHON	Austin	AB	278	27	Ireland	01/07/1800	01/07/1800	Former Books
LANG	Joseph	AB	257	39	Surry	01/07/1800	01/07/1800	Former Books
LANG	John	Drummer	4		Royal Marines	01/07/1800	01/07/1800	Former Books
LAUNDERS	James	LM	29	41	Chatham	01/07/1800	01/07/1800	Former Books
LAUROSE	Martin	Ord.	376	24	Quebec	01/07/1800	01/07/1800	Former Books
LAWRENCE	Gregy.	Master At Arms	175	35	Whitcomb	01/07/1800	01/07/1800	Former Books
LAY	Henry	LM	205	22	Efsex	01/07/1800	01/07/1800	Former Books

Surname	First	Qualities	No.	Age	Born	Entered	Appeared	Previous
LEE	Thomas	Ord.	290	24	Reading	01/07/1800	01/07/1800	Former Books
LESLIE	Alex.	AB	238	24	Newcastle	01/07/1800	01/07/1800	Former Books
LEWIS	George	AB	77	40	Stone Kent	01/07/1800	01/07/1800	Former Books
Slain in fight with the enemy 02/04/1801								
LEWIS	John	QrtrGnr	472	29	Exeter	01/07/1800	01/07/1800	Former Books
LEWIS	William	Lieut.	16			01/07/1800	01/07/1800	Former Books
LEWIS	William	Pte.RM	49			01/07/1800	01/07/1800	Former Books
LIGHTON	Thomas	AB	251	37	Chatham	01/07/1800	01/07/1800	Former Books
LILLY	James	AB	279	23	Stamford	01/07/1800	01/07/1800	Former Books
LOVELL	James Cook	Captain's	158	25	Reading	01/07/1800	01/07/1800	Former Books
LOVELL	John	Boy	BBB7	13	London	01/07/1800	01/07/1800	Former Books
LUCHARS	Andw.	Ord.	333	25	Perth	01/07/1800	01/07/1800	Former Books

Surname	First	Qualities	No.	Age	Born	Entered	Appeared	Previous
LUMPHRY	William	Ord.	98	23	Cornwall	01/07/1800	01/07/1800	Former books
LYFORD	Henry	Lieut.	360	Commissioned		01/07/1800	01/07/1800	Former Books
LYNN*	Mattw.	LM	462	20	London	01/07/1800	01/07/1800	Former Books
MACKIE	Andw.	Ord.	72	25	Couey?	01/07/1800	01/07/1800	Former Books
MADDIN	Patk.	LM	463	19	Roscommon	01/07/1800	01/07/1800	Former Books
MADSON	Kenneth	AB	280	50	Scotland	01/07/1800	01/07/1800	Former Books
MAINES	John	Pte.RM	51			01/07/1800	01/07/1800	Former Books
MAITLAND	John	Pte.RM	131			26/12/1800	26/12/1800	Plymouth HQ
MALPAS	Louise	Pte.RM	8			01/07/1800	01/07/1800	Former Books
MANNING	Richd.	Pte.RM	104			24/07/1800	24/07/1800	Plymouth HQ
MANNING	Saml.	LM	444	20	N.Yarmouth	01/07/1800	01/07/1800	Former Books
MANSELL*	Thos.	Mid.	352	15	Iscoad	01/07/1800	01/07/1800	Former Books

Surname	First	Qualities	No.	Age	Born	Entered	Appeared	Previous
MARK	James	Yeoman Powder Room	50	45	Portsoy	01/07/1800	01/07/1800	Former Books
MARKHAM	John	Boy	BBB1	13	London	01/07/1800	01/07/1800	Former Books
MARKHAM	Willm.	AB Quarter Gunner 01/09/1800	37	41	Hull	01/07/1800	01/07/1800	Former Books
Will and power of attorney to wife 20th March 1800								
MARLINE	Edwd.	Ord.	287	24	Ireland	01/07/1800	01/07/1800	Former Books
MARTIN	James	AB	274	30	Plymouth	01/07/1800	01/07/1800	Former Books
MARTIN	Rich.	AB	264	20	Devon	01/07/1800	01/07/1800	Former Books
MASON	James	AB	87	53	Queensferry	01/07/1800	01/07/1800	Former Books
MASON	Robt.W	Stewards Mate	32	20	Chatham	01/07/1800	01/07/1800	Former Books
MASTERMAN	Thos.	Quarter Master	160	35	York	01/07/1800	01/07/1800	Former Books
MATTHEWS	Thomas	Ord.	116	29	Norwich	01/07/1800	01/07/1800	Former Books

Surname	First	Qualities	No.	Age	Born	Entered	Appeared	Previous
MAUBLEY	Edwd.	Pte RM	11			01/07/1800	01/07/1800	Former Books
MAUNDERS	Richd.	Ord.	121	20	Fireshire	01/07/1800	01/07/1800	Former Books
MAXLEY	Mattw.	LM	450	40	Blakeney	01/07/1800	01/07/1800	Former Books
MAYBROOK	John	Ord.	334	20	London	01/07/1800	01/07/1800	Former Books
MAYES	Mattw.	Pte RM	24			01/07/1800	01/07/1800	Former Books
MEFSINGHAM	Michl.	AB	52	26	Sunderland	01/07/1800	01/07/1800	Former Books
MERCHANT	Willm.	Pte.RM	125			26/12/1800	26/12/1800	Plymouth HQ
MEREDEW	Thos.	AB	255	29	London	01/07/1800	01/07/1800	Former Books
MEREFIELD	Abram.	Arm?	230	53	Gosport	01/07/1800	01/07/1800	Former books
McCARTHY	Edwd.	Ord.	85	36	London	01/07/1800	01/07/1800	Former Books
McCARTY	Dens.	Pte.RM	84			01/07/1800	01/07/1800	Former Books
McCORMICK	Jas.	Ord.	328	21	Dendock	01/07/1800	01/07/1800	Former Books

Surname	First	Qualities	No.	Age	Born	Entered	Appeared	Previous
McCORMICK	Thos.	LM	193	30	Ireland	01/07/1800	01/07/1800	Former Books
McDERMOTT	Robt.	LM	503	26	Dublin	01/07/1800	29/07/1800	Beaulieu HS
McDONALD	Dunc.	AB	366	45	Argyleshire	01/07/1800	01/07/1800	Former Books
McGILL	William	Ord.	28	29	Chatham	01/07/1800	01/07/1800	Former Books
McKIRKNER	John	Pte RM	6			01/07/1800	01/07/1800	Former Books
McLANE	John	LM	208	31	London	01/07/1800	01/07/1800	Former Books
McNAMARA	Michl.	Ord.	414	21	Limerick	01/07/1800	01?07/1800	Former Books
MIDDLETON	James	Quarter Masters Mate 02/04/01 Midshipman	156	20	N.Britain	01/07/1800	01/07/1800	Former Books
MILES	William	Ord.	431	25	Cornwall	01/07/1800	01/07/1800	Former Books
MILLER	Robert	LM	111	38	Chigwell	01/07/1800	01/07/1800	Former Books
MILLS	John	LM	461	25	Reading	01/07/1800	01/07/1800	Former Books

Surname	First	Qualities	No.	Age Born	Entered	Appeared	Previous
MILNE*	William	Mid.	345	16 Carron	01/07/1800	01/07/1800	Former Books
MITCHELL	Hugh	Boatswain	527	Warrant 21/12/00	16/01/1800	16/10/1800	Excellent
MITCHELL	Isaac	LM Carpenters Crew 01/09/1800	465	20 London	01/07/1800	01/07/1800	Former Books
MITCHELL	Thomas	Pte.RM	64		01/07/1800	01/07/1800	Former Books
MONKS	John	AB Ord. 01/11/1800	405	27 Dublin	01/07/1800	01/07/1800	Former Books
MOORE	John	Pte.RM	127		26/12/1800	26/12/1800	Plymouth HQ
MOORE(1)	William	LM	25	42 Harrison	01/07/1800	01/07/1800	Former Books
MOORE(2)	William	LM	206	20 Buckingham	01/07/1800	01/07/1800	Former Books
MORRIS	Thomas	Boy	BB18	12 Haverfordwest	15/12/1800	13/03/1801	Vol. Holden
MORRIS	John	Pte.RM	105		20/09/1800	20/09/1800	Plymouth HQ
MOSELY	Saml.	Pte.RM	88		01/07/1800	01/07/1800	Former Books

Surname	First	Qualities	No.	Age	Born	Entered	Appeared	Previous
MOSELY	William	Ord	96	40	Bermingham	01/07/1800	01/07/1800	Former Books
MURPHY	Thos.	Pte.RM	39			01/07/1800	01/07/1800	Former Books
Discharged dead 02/04/1801 slain in fight								
MURRY	William	Sailmkr	233	25	Dundee	01/07/1800	01/07/1800	Former Books
MYATT	Edmond	Boy	BBB13	13	Staffordshire	01/07/1800	01/07/1800	Former Books
NASH	James	Pte.RM	107			20/09/1800	20/09/1800	Plymouth HQ
NASH	Rich	Boy	BB19	14	Haverfordwest	09/12/1800	13/03/1801	Vol. Holden
NELSON	Aaron	Pte RM	15			01/07/1800	01/07/1800	Former Books
NELSON The R.Hon.Lord Nelson Vice Adml. of the Blue						26/03/1801	26/03/1801	St. George
Discharged 02/04/1801 St. George								
NICHOLS	Thos.	Pte.RM	56			01/07/1800	01/07/1800	Former Books
NICOLL	Andw.	AB	67	30	Dysart	01/07/1800	01/07/1800	Former Books
NICHOLS	Edwd.	LM	191	24	London	01/07/1800	01/07/1800	Former Books

Surname	First	Qualities	No.	Age	Born	Entered	Appeared	Previous
NORMAN	Robt.	Ord.	94	56	Bristol	01/07/1800	01/07/1800	Former Books
NORTH	Joseph	Ord.	346	22	Lincoln	01/07/1800	01/07/1800	Former Books
O'BRIEN	Thos.	AB	534	22	Ireland	03/01/1800	09/03/1800	R. William
ODLANDS	James	LM	187	26	London	01/07/1880	01/07/1800	Former Books
ORAM	Charles	Mid.	339	18	Wiltshire	01/07/1800	01/07/1800	Former Books
ORMOND	James	LM	470	18	Stroud	01/07/1800	01/07/1800	Former Books
OTTY	William	Pte.RM	48			01/07/1800	01/07/1800	Former Books
OWENS	John	Ord.	113	37	London	01/07/1800	01/07/1800	Former Books
PADOA	Joseph	Boy	B10	14	Malta	01/07/1800	01/07/1800	Former Books
PADOA*	Pascal	Boy	BBB5	13	Malta	01/07/1800	01/07/1800	Former Books
PAGE	James	Ord.	31	26	Maidstone	01/07/1800	01/07/1800	Former Books
PAGE	Joseph	AB	370	24	Emsworth	01/07/1800	01/07/1800	Former Books

Surname	First	Qualities	No.	Age	Born	Entered	Appeared	Previous
PAINE	Richard	Pte.RM	113			26/12/1800	26/12/1800	Plymouth HQ
PALMER	Fran.	LM	215	50	Maidstone	01/07/1800	01/07/1800	Former Books
PARRY	Edwd.	Boy	BB17	12	Haverfordwest	16/11/1800	13/03/1801	Vol. Holden
PATE	William	LM	184	25	London	01/07/1800	01/07/1800	Former Books
PATTERSON	Hans.	Quarter Gunner	150	36	Norway	01/07/1800	01/07/1800	Former Books
PATTERSON	John	AB Carpenters Crew 01/09/1800	356	23	Berwick	01/07/1800	01/07/1800	Former Books
PATTIN	John	LM	445	25	Dundee	01/07/1800	01/07/1800	Former Books
PAYNE	William	Ord.	314	23	Exeter	01/07/1800	01/07/1800	Former Books
PEARCE	Mark	Ord. AB 01/11/1800	430	21	Hampshire	01/07/1800	01/07/1800	Former Books
PEARSON*	Hugh	Lieut.	518		Commission	02/10/1800	02/10/1800	Comsn

Surname	First	Qualities	No.	Age	Born	Entered	Appeared	Previous
PEERS	Thomas	Capt.RM	26			01/07/1800	01/07/1800	Former Books
PEGG	William	Pte.RM	70			01/07/1800	01/07/1800	Former Books
PENGELLY	Willm.	Pte.RM	106			20/09/1800	20/09/1800	Plymouth HQ
PENNY	Saml.	Pte.RM	130			26/12/1800	26/12/1800	Plymouth HQ
PEPLOW	Thomas	Pte.RM	87			01/07/1800	01/07/1800	Former Books
PICKARD	Joseph	Boy	BBB11	13	London	01/07/1800	01/07/1800	Former Books
PINGRAY	Frans.	LM	448	45	Malta	01/07/1800	01/07/1800	Former Books
PLUNKETT	John	LM	459	27	Ireland	01/07/1800	01/07/1800	Former Books
PLUNKETT	Richd.	Ord.	234	25	Pembroke	01/07/1800	01/07/1800	Former Books
POORE	James	Carptnrs Mate	161	27	Ireland	01/07/1800	01/07/1800	Former Books
POPE	James	Pte.RM	121			26/12/1800	25/12/1800	Plymouth HQ

Surname	First	Qualities	No.	Age	Born	Entered	Appeared	Previous
POPE	John	Pte.RM	120			01/07/1800	01/07/1800	Former Books
PORTELLI*	Bernd.	LM	540	57	Malta	11/03/1801	11/03/1801	1st Class Boys
POTTER	Thomas	Quarter Gunner	39	31	Grimsby	01/07/1800	01/07/1800	Former Books
POWER	Thomas	Quarter	169	27	Devon	01/07/1800	01/07/1800	Former Books
POWER	Willm.	Ord. AB 01/09/1800	495	27	Waterford	09/07/1800	09/07/1800	Prest
POWRIE	William	AB	371	29	Bristol	01/07/1800	01/07/1800	Former Books
PRIEST	Thomas	Ord.	379	40	Ware	01/07/1800	01/07/1800	Former Books
PURVIS	Alex.	Quarter Masters Mate	163	30	Berwick	01/07/1800	01/07/1800	Former Books
QUINN	Patk.	LM	507	20	Co. Derry	06/05/1800	20/07/1800	Beaulieu HS
RAGGETT	Richd.	Pte.RM	90			01/07/1800	01/07/1800	Former Books

Surname	First	Qualities	No.	Age	Born	Entered	Appeared	Previous
RAINBOLT	Hans.	Ord.	418	20	Prufsia	01/07/1800	01/07/1800	Former Books
RAY	William	Ord.	301	27	Belfast	01/07/1800	01/07/1800	Former Books
READ	George	Carpntrs Crew 01/09/1800 Corporal	102	29	Isle of Wight	01/07/1800	01/07/1800	Former Books
READ*	Thomas	LM	180	20	Chatham	01/07/1800	01/07/1800	Former Books
REBECCA	William	Yeoman Sheets	101	54	Newcastle	01/07/1800	01/07/1800	Former Books
RENTOUL	Alex.	AB	64	25	Pathead	01/07/1800	01/07/1800	Former Books
REX	George	Pte.RM	128			26/12/1800	26/12/1800	Plymouth HQ
RICE	Edmond	Ord.	71	39	Glamorgan	01/07/1800	01/07/1800	Former Books
RICE	Edward	AB Ord. 01/11/1800	406	22	Dublin	01/07/1800	01/07/1800	Former Books
RICHARDS	Willm.	Pte RM	13			01/07/1800	01/07/1800	Former Books

Surname	First	Qualities	No.	Age	Born	Entered	Appeared	Previous
ROACH	James	AB	375	32	Cork	01/07/1800	01/07/1800	Former Books
ROBERTS	Thomas	AB	282	20	Greenwich	01/07/1800	01/07/1800	Former Books
ROBERTSON	Lewis	AB	105	27	Guinea	01/07/1800	01/07/1800	Former Books
ROFS	William	AB	240	32	N.America	01/07/1800	01/07/1800	Former Books
ROGERS	George	Pte RM	20			01/07/1800	01/07/1800	Former Books
ROGERS	Simon	Pte RM	22			01/07/1800	01/07/1800	Former Books
ROWE	Thomas	LM	433	20	London	01/07/1800	01/07/1800	Former Books
RUFSELL	Willm.	Pte.RM	43			01/07/1800	01/07/1800	Former Books
RYAN	Michl.	LM	457	30	Cork	01/07/1800	01/07/1800	Former Books
SALMON	Peter	Ord.	317	20	Jersey	01/07/1800	01/07/1800	Former Books
SATCHELL	Chas.	Ord.	127	22	Wicklow	01/07/1800	01/07/1800	Former Books
SCOFIELD	Edw.	AB	386	40	Lancashire	01/07/1800	01/07/1800	Former Books

Surname	First	Qualities	No.	Age	Born	Entered	Appeared	Previous
SCOTT	John	AB	531	23	Hull	03/01/1800	09/03/1800	R.William
SCOTT	Robert	Quarter Gunner	162	40	Pomona Orkneys	01/07/1800	01/07/1800	Former Books
SCOTT	William	Ord.	315	??	Whitehaven	01/07/1800	01/07/1800	Former Books
SEARLE	John	Yeoman	154	39	Devon	01/07/1800	01/07/1800	Former Books
Will & power to wife 14/03/1800 Powder Room								
SENNELL	Rich.	Mid.	517	24	S. Wales	20/09/1800	20/09/1800	Volunteer
SERRARD	Julian	LM	435	40	St. Lucia	01/07/1800	01/07/1800	Former Books
SEYBINE	Joseph	Ord.	306	21	Liverpool	01/07/1800	01/07/1800	Former Books
SHANNO	Nichs.	Pte RM	21			01/07/1800	01/07/1800	Former Books
SHEANE	Danl.	AB 01/11/00 Ord. 01/03/01 AB	349	30	Cork	01/07/1800	01/07/1800	Former Books
SHEPPARD	Jethro	AB Ord 01/11/1800	401	39	Wareham Dorset	01/07/1800	01/07/1800	Former Books

Surname	First	Qualities	No.	Age	Born	Entered	Appeared	Previous
SHERLOCK	John	Carps. Crew	18	26	Woolwich	01/07/1800	01/07/1800	Former Books
SHILLING	James	AB	256	32	Kent	01/07/1800	01/07/1800	Former Books
SHORT	Chris.	Gunners Mate	283	41	Hexham	01/07/1800	01/07/1800	Former Books
SIMMS	Charles	Pte.RM	102			24/07/1800	24/07/1800	Plymouth HQ
SIMMS	James	Ord.	82	23	Dundee	01/07/1800	01/07/1800	Former Books
SIMONS	James	Carpentr	321	By warrant		01/07/1800	01/07/1800	Former Books
SIMPSON	George	AB	258	43	Whitby	01/07/1800	01/07/1800	Former Books
		01/09/1800 Quarter Gunner 02/04/1801 Midshipman						
SKEATER	Charles	LM	441	23	Lambeth	01/07/1800	01/07/1800	Former Books
SLATER	James	Quarter Master	153	26	Lincoln	01/07/1800	01/07/1800	Former Books
SLATER	William	Volunteer B	14	16	Plymouth	10/03/1801	10/03/1801	2nd Class Boys

Surname	First	Qualities	No.	Age	Born	Entered	Appeared	Previous
SMALL	Soloman	Ord.	40	49	Rivey, Lincs.	01/07/1800	01/07/1800	Former Books
SMITH	Jasper	Ord.	415	19	Edingburgh	01/07/1800	01/07/1800	Former Books
SMITH(1)	John	Ord.	75	24	Nottingly	01/07/1800	01/07/1800	Former Books
SMITH	Thomas	Corp.RM	111			26/12/1800	26/12/1800	Plymouth HQ
SMITH	William	Armrs. Mate	24	24	London	01/07/1800	01/07/1800	Former Books
SMITH	Willm.	AB	539	40	Lincolnshire	23/02/1801	09/03/1801	Vol. Rendezvous
SMITH	Vengonso	LM	481	18	Malta	01/07/1800	01/07/1800	Former Books
SOLLEY	George	AB	381	30	Canterbury	01/07/1800	01/07/1800	Former Books
SOUTH	William	AB	48	20	Hull	01/07/1800	01/07/1800	Former Books
SPRAIN	Jacob	Pte.RM	54			01/07/1800	01/07/1800	Former Books
STANMORE	John	Pte.RM	119			26/12/1800	26/12/1800	Plymouth HQ

Surname	First	Qualities	No.	Age	Born	Entered	Appeared	Previous
STEEL	James	Yeoman Sheets	171	37	Scotland	01/07/1800	01/07/1800	Former Books
STEPHENSON*	James	LM	209	25	Ireland	01/07/1800	01/07/1800	Former Books
STEPHENSON	Joseph	LM	217	33	Yorkshire	01/07/1800	01/07/1800	Former Books
STOKES	William	Ord.	319	16	Durham	01/07/1800	01/07/1800	Former Books
STONE	Joseph	AB Ord 01/11/1800	402	25	Worcester	01/07/1800	01/07/1800	Former Books
STOREY	Jacob	Quarter Gunner	337	35	Newcastle	01/07/1800	01/07/1800	Former Books
STRACHEN	Peter	School-Master	143	26	Bethnl Green	01/07/1800	01/07/1800	Former Books
STREET	John	Quarter Gunner	536	34	Dawlish	03/01/1800	09/03/1800	R. William
STUART	John	AB	262	24	Ireland	01/07/1800	01/07/1800	Former Books

Surname	First	Qualities	No.	Age	Born	Entered	Appeared	Previous
SULLIVAN	Chas.	LM	220	46	Cork	01/07/1800	01/07/1800	Former Books
SULLIVAN	William	AB	281	36	Cork	01/07/1800	01/07/1800	Former Books
SWAN	Edwd.	Ord.	125	27	Dublin	01/07/1800	01/07/1800	Former Books
SWANWICK	Willm.	LM	130	47	London	01/07/1800	01/07/1800	Former Books
SWIFT	John D.	AB	49	45	London	01/07/1800	01/07/1800	Former Books
TAYLOR	David	SgtRM	2			01/07/1800	01/07/1800	Former Books
TAYLOR(1)	John	AB	79	22	Durham	01/07/1800	01/07/1800	Former Books
TAYLOR(3)	John	AB	305	24	Bristol	01/07/1800	01/07/1800	Former Books
TAYLOR(4)	John	LM	424	19	Lincolnshire	01/07/1800	01/07/1800	Former Books
TAYLOR	Thomas	AB	261	24	Berks.	01/07/1800	01/07/1800	Former Books
THACKER	Benj.	Boy	BBB14	14	London	01/07/1800	01/07/1800	Former Books
THACKERY	George	LM	446	26	Yorkshire	01/07/1800	01/07/1800	Former Books

Surname	First	Qualities	No.	Age	Born	Entered	Appeared	Previous
THOMAS	James	AB Mid. 02/04/1801	248	23	Portland USA	01/07/1800	01/07/1800	Former Books
THOMAS	John	LM	188	22	London	01/07/1800	01/07/1800	Former Books
THOMAS	William	Pte.RM	66			01/07/1800	01/07/1800	Former Books
THOMPSON	Benj.	Mid.	516	15	Plymouth	19/09/1800	30/09/1800	1st Class Boys
THOMPSON Discharged 06/04/01 invalided	John	Gnner	9		By Warrant	01/07/1800	01/07/1800	Former Books
THOMPSON	Peter	Ord.	419	23	Denmark	01/07/1800	01/07/1800	Former Books
THOMPSON	Willm.	Volunteer	B10	14	Plymouth	21/07/1801	21/07/1801	2nd Class Boys
TILLMAN	Peter	Volunteer	B12	15	Plymouth	10/03/1801	10/03/1801	2nd Class Boys
TITUS?	John	Ord.	286	25	Brompton	01/07/1800	01/07/1800	Former Books
TODD	John	Acting Surgeon's Mate	529			05/02/1800	05/02/1800	

Surname	First	Qualities	No.	Age	Born	Entered	Appeared	Previous
TRESER	Godlip	Pte.RM	114			26/12/1800	26/12/1800	Plymouth HQ
TRUFS	John	Pte.rm	59			01/07/1800	01/07/1800	Former books
TUCKER	John	LM	451	21	London	01/07/1800	01/07/1800	Former Books
TUCKFIELD	John	AB Ord. 01/11/1800	519	23	Cornwall	10/07/1800	10/07/1800	
UPTON	Thomas	LM	189	37	Maidstone	01/07/1800	01/07/1800	Former Books
VAUGHAN	William	Ord.	335	21	Bristol	01/07/1800	01/07/1800	Former Books
VELLAI	Gabriel	LM	525	17	Malta	20/11/1800	20/11/1800	2nd Class Boys
VENN	Willm.	Pte.RM	108			20/09/1800	20/09/1800	Plymouth HQ
WALKER	David	AB Quarter Gunner 01/11/1800 Boatswains Mate 09/04/01	484	27	Newcastle	01/07/1800	01/07/1800	Former Books
WALKER	Mattw.	Mid.	159	29	Newcastle	01/07/1800	01/07/1800	Former Books
WALKING	Henry	Pte.RM	79			01/07/1800	01/07/1800	Former Books

Surname	First	Qualities	No.	Age	Born	Entered	Appeared	Previous
WALLAS	Thomas	Secretary to Lord Nelson				26/03/1801	26/03/1801	St. George
Discharged 02/04/1801 St. George								
WALLS	John	AB	395	36	Marchwood Hants	01/07/1800	01/07/1800	Former Books
WARD	William	AB	239	33	Coventry	01/07/1800	01/07/1800	Former Books
Will & power of Atty 7th March 1800								
WARDROPE	James	Cook	11			01/07/1800	01/07/1800	Former Books
WATSON	Adam	LM	63	22	Kircaldie	01/07/1800	01/07/1800	Former Books
WATSON	John	Quarter Gunner	167	45	Edingburgh	01/07/1800	01/07/1800	Former Books
WATSON	John	Pte.RM	123			26/12/1800	26/12/1800	Plymouth HQ
WATTS	WB	2nd LieutRM				01/07/1800	01/07/1800	Former Books
WEBB	Fredk.P	AB	247	31	Ireland	01/07/1800	01/07/1800	Former books

Surname	First	Qualities	No.	Age	Born	Entered	Appeared	Previous
WELLS(1)	Thomas	Quarter Gunner	38	27	Grimsby	01/07/1800	01/07/1800	Former Books
WELLS(2)	Thomas	Ord.	117	26	Gillingham	01/07/1800	01/07/1800	Former Books
WELSH	Patk.	Ord.	493	18	Waterford	21/06/1800	01/07/1800	Beaulieu Chatham HS
WHEELER	John	Pte.RM	44			01/07/1800	01/07/1800	Former Books
WHERELAND	Geo.	LM	455	21	Cork	01/07/1800	01/07/1800	Former Books
WHITE	Charles	Gunners Mate	172	43	N. Britain	01/07/1800	01/07/1800	Former Books
WHITE*	James	Pte.RM	41			01/07/1800	01/07/1800	Former Books
WHITE	John	AB	260	20	Windsor	01/07/1800	01/07/1800	Former Books
WHITE(2)	John	LM	432	25	Devonshire	01/07/1800	01/07/1800	Former Books
WHITE	William	AB Ord. 01/11/1800	475	22	Pool	01/07/1800	01/07/1800	Former Books

Surname	First	Qualities	No.	Age	Born	Entered	Appeared	Previous
WHITHERS	John	Pte.RM	103			24/07/1800	24/07/1800	Plymouth HQ
WICKERS	William	Ord.	118	24	Gillingham	01/07/1800	01/07/1800	Former Books
WIDDOST	Robt.	Ord.	90	29	Ireland	01/07/1800	01/07/1800	Former Books
WIGGINS	Thomas	LM	19	22	London	01/07/1800	01/07/1800	Former Books
WILKINSON	Wm.	Lieut	1			01/07/1800	01/07/1800	Former Books
WILLCOX	Edward	QrtrGnr	41	51	Hammersmith	01/07/1800	01/07/1800	Former Books
Power of attorney to Wife 16 Jan 1801								
WILLIAMS	Edwd.	Coxwain	141	27	Bristol	01/07/1800	01/07/1800	Former Books
WILLIAMS	Fredk.	LM	458	22	Sweden	01/07/1800	01/07/1800	Former Books
WILLIAMS	John	AB	133	24	Barry Glamorgan	01/07/1800	01/07/1800	Former Books
WILLSON	James M	Ord.	97	24	New Molton Yorks	01/07/1800	01/07/1800	Former Books

Surname	First	Qualities	No.	Age	Born	Entered	Appeared	Previous
WILLSON	Saml.	LM	437	25	Norway	01/07/1800	01/07/1800	Former Books
WILLTON	Richd.	Ord.	123	40	Bath	01/07/1800	01/07/1800	Former Books
WINN	John	LM	498	20	Exeter	19/07/1800	19/07/1800	Ethalion
WISE	John	AB	42	20	Prussia	01/07/1800	01/07/1800	Former Books
WOODCOCK	James	Pte.RM	116			26/12/1800	26/12/1800	Plymouth HQ
WORKMAN	John	Pte.RM	61			01/07/1800	01/07/1800	Former Books
WRATSON	John	Swabber	242	40	Rosherithen	01/07/1800	01/07/1800	Former Books
WRIGHT	Richd.	Pte RM	12			01/07/1800	01/07/1800	Former Books
WYATT	Willm.	M Mid.	511	14	London	01/08/1800	01/08/1800	1st Class Boys
YOULDEN Discharged Dead 02/04/01 Slain in fight	Henry	Mstrs. Mate	140	24	Brixham	01/07/1800	01/07/1800	Former Books

* indicates the issue of the Naval General Service Medal

NOTES OF INTEREST FROM THE MUSTER

Nationalities

The 'where born' column of the muster includes references to: - Constantinople, Ajaccio, Sweden, Naples, Hamburgh, Malta, Trieste, Portugal, America, Prussia and 'At sea' (further confirmation of women carried on board?)
One of the seamen THOMPSON is shown as having been born in Denmark.

Age range

12 – 57 years
Average age of seamen 28.6 years.
Mix of Qualities - Landsmen 97 – Ordinary 104 – Able Seamen 122

The following named were also listed on the muster - being carried as supernumeries until the end of hostilities. With time to make preparations it is of interest that a group of signalmen were carried over from the *St. George*, presumably to assist in the signalling from the commander in the *Elephant* to his squadron.
Midshipman Gill from the *London* was subsequently listed as one of the wounded from the *Elephant*.

Surname	**First**	**Qualities No.**	**Age Born**	**Entered**	**Appeared**	**Previous**
ALLEN	Thos.	Servnt 243		25/03/01	25/03/01	St. George
BALL	Willm.	Signlmn 238		25/03/01	25/03/01	St. George
BEHAMY	John	Signlmn 234		25/03/01	25/03/01	St. George
BRIGGS	Barnet	Signlmn 233		25/03/01	25/03/01	St. George
ELLIS	William	Pilot 228		15/03/01	15/03/01	London
JACKSON	Charles	Signlmn 235		25/03/01	25/03/01	St. George
GILL	Rs.	Mid. 241		26103/01	26/03/01	London
HOWARD	J.	Servnt 244		26/03/01	26/03/01	London
LANGFORD	Fredk.	Lieut. 240		25/03/01	25/03/01	London

Surname	First	Qualities No.	Age Born	Entered	Appeared	Previous
THYNE	Robt.	Signlmn 236		25/03/01	25/03/01	St. George
USHER	John	Signlmn 239		25/03/01	23/03/01	St. George
WHITE	George	Sergnt. 242		26/03/01	26/03/01	London
WILLIAMS	Joseph	Signlmn 237		25/03/01	25/03/01	St. George

The Rifle Corps At Copenhagen

"It has invariably been the object of great commanders to mingle authority with lenity, to inspire their troops with confidence in their own capacity, to call forth their enthusiasm, and create a common feeling between the officer and the soldier. Upon these principles, Fredrick, Suvarrov and the great Nelson acted, and we need not cite further examples."

Colonel Stewart

The Rifle Corps at Copenhagen

Formation of the Regiment

Raised as the Experimental Corps of Riflemen in 1800

Served with Nelson at Copenhagen in 1801

Became the 95th or Rifle Regiment in 1803

Fought throughout the Peninsular war brigaded with the 43rd and 52nd Regiments as the Light Brigade, and later in 1810 as the immortal Light Division under the command of Robert Crawford

After the battle of Waterloo restyled "THE RIFLE BRIGADE" and removed from the line as a mark of distinction 1816

THE RIFLE CORPS

Raised in 1800 the RIFLE CORPS. won it's first battle honour Copenhagen serving in the Baltic expedition led by Admiral Sir Hyde Parker in April 1801. The Hon.Col.William Stewart, co-founder and commander of the Rifle Corps,.had been chosen to lead the military element of what was essentially a naval expedition. His force comprised of 750 men of the 49th Regiment and a detachment of the Rifle Corps. These riflemen men, numbering 115 in total, were under the command of Captain Thomas Sidney Beckwith.

They were armed with the new Baker Rifle, invented by Ezekiel Baker, gunmaker to His Majesty George III. This well known craftsman had won the competition, based on practical trials, to find a suitable rifle for the new Rifle Corps. The new gun, incorporating a thirty inch barrel, was rifled with seven grooves with a quarter turn over it's length. These spiraling grooves were sufficient to spin the bullet, and achieve a remarkable accuracy. In the hands of the newly trained Rifle Corps they would prove to be a deadly weapon.

The Corps embarked at Portsmouth on the 28th of February 1801 on board *St. George*, bearing the flag of Lord Nelson who was second in command of the fleet. On arriving at Yarmouth from where the expedition would depart, half a company of riflemen were transferred to *London*, flagship of the Commander in Chief Sir Hyde Parker.

In Yarmouth Col. Stewart wrote urgently to the Ordnance storekeeper for the delivery of ammunition for his troops, this included, *99000 musquet ball cartridges, 4000 musquet flints, 10,000 carbine ball cartridges, 6 reams of cartridge paper for carbine ammunition,* and to include,a *number of spikes for spiking guns* along with *entrenching tools for a hundred men.* These latter items on Col. Stewart's list signified Lord Nelson's intended task for the infantry, should storming the Crown Battery become practicable later on.

On the 12th of March, the fleet left Yarmouth Roads reaching the northern point of Denmark on the 19th, and later, dropping down the sound anchored 5 miles above Copenhagen on the 26th. The same evening Lord Nelson removed his flag from the *St. George*, to a lighter ship the *Elephant 74*, accompanied by Col. Stewart, Captain Beckwith, and his riflemen. The remaining riflemen under the command of the Adjutant, Lieutenant Grant, were transferred from Admiral Sir Hyde Parker's flagship to the *Isis 50.* The detachment of the 49th Regiment were then distributed amongst the other ships of the line. With Nelson's plan to attack from the south adopted, on April 1st he took up his position and moored two miles to the south of the nearest Danish ship.

It was arranged that flat bottomed boats, manned and armed would remain on the sheltered side of each battle ship as they formed their line of baffle. These boats would carry the troops in their assault on the Crown batteries in the event of the Danish ships surrendering or being captured. Meanwhile, fully armed the soldiers would keep up a barrage of musket and rifle fire from the upperworks of the ships.

Col. Stewart's well known account of the battle, repeated elsewhere, indicates the ferocity of the struggle, for nearly three hours the pounding continued, the Rifle Corps contributing both with their Baker rifle's and by manning the guns along side the gun crews of the *Elephant* and the *Isis*. Both Colonel Stewart and Captain Beckwith shared the honour of being present on the deck of the *Elephant* when at approximately 1 pm the famous signal No. 39 (break off action) was shown aboard the *London*, Hyde Parker's flagship, and both were witness to Lord Nelson's decision to acknowledge the signal but to ignore it, and to continue flying No. 16 (close action).

At the close of the battle Lord Nelson in his famous dispatch stated: 'The honourable Colonel Stewart did me the favour to be on board the *Elephant* and himself, with every officer and soldier under his orders, shared with the pleasure the toils and the dangers of the day'.

Sadly the action was not without cost to the soldiers who had shared in those toils and dangers. Lieutenant Grant, the Adjutant of the Rifle Corps, was killed whilst serving the quarterdeck guns of the *Isis*; he was the first officer of the Rifle Corps to be killed in action. Colonel Stewart later recommended that Grant's 1st Lieutenancy in the Rifle Corps be passed on the 2nd Lieutenant Prendergast, who had commanded a division of the Rifle Company with great spirit during the remainder of the action. Also aboard the *Isis* a further two riflemen were killed and two wounded. Aboard the *Elephant* a volunteer of the Cornwall Miners, Captain James Bawden, who was serving with the Rifle Corps was killed, and two riflemen wounded.

Captain Beckwith, who would later command a Brigade in the Peninsula, and would go on to command the regiment, would never forget being present on the deck of the *Elephant* with Lord Nelson during the thick of the battle, and as the letter (opposite) indicates, writes with pride of the occasion.

On the 25th of the April Admiral Sir Hyde Parker was superseded, and Lord Nelson given command of the fleet. He immediately weighed anchor and sailed for Revel to engage the Russians. The Rifle Corps accompanied him throughout his Baltic cruise, during which peace was concluded with Russia and the Northern Confederacy finally broken up. At the end of June, Nelson returned to England and there Colonel Stewart and the Rifle Corps rejoined the rest of the Regiment at Weymouth.

When Stewart's report of the battle was received at Horse Guards. A letter ordered by the commander-in-chief HRH The Duke of York was sent in reply, dated April 22nd 1801, this letter reflected the royal approbation of the gallantry and good conduct of the officers and men of the 49th Regiment, and the detachment of the Rifle Corps. His Majesty expressed him personal thanks and gratitude by promoting Stewart to full Colonel.

Lord Nelson's regard for Colonel Stewart had increased throughout the Copenhagen campaign and a warm friendship ensued, echoed by the tone of their continuing correspondence and Nelson's keen interest in the development of the Rifle Corps.

Lord Nelson's unremitting struggle for recognition in the form of medals (referred to elsewhere), for the officer's who so valiantly served him at Copenhagen, included Stewart, but to no avail. Stewart entered into correspondence with St. Vincent in his own right, on the same issue, some twenty years later.

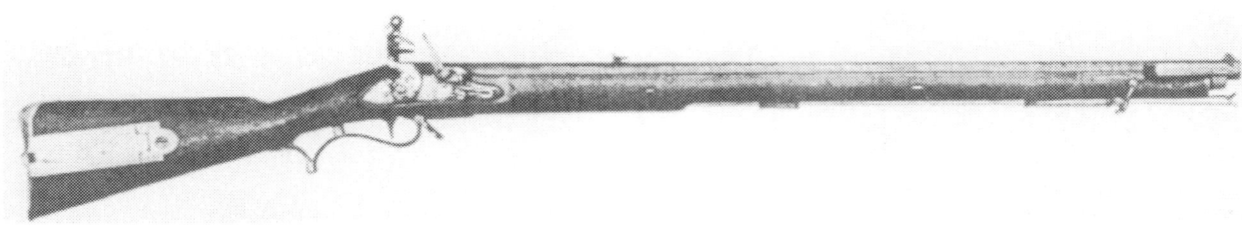

The Baker Rifle

LETTER FROM CAPTAIN SIDNEY BECKWITH – RIFLE CORPS
(Original letter by kind permission of the Sim Comfort Collection)

"HM Ship Elephant off Copenhagen
April 5 1801

My Dear Sir:

From your long kindness and Friendship I am led to believe that you will not be sorry to hear it was my good fortune to be in Lord Nelson's Ship in our hard fought action of yesterday.

Independent of other considerations my curiosity was extreme to be an eye witness of the conduct of such a character in action. Most amply was that curiosity satisfied. Nor can I conceive anything more perfect than every part of the fine little Hero's conduct on that trying occasion.

For some time (more than two hours) the defense made by the Danes was so obstinate that Sir Hyde Parker made the signal to discontinue the action. With this his Lordship refused to comply, observing, his Enemy were gallant fellows, but if he could not beat them in two hours he must take three, or if that would not do, he must take four hours to do it. This determination saves us from destruction as well as from disgrace, since on the actions ceasing, three of our line of Battle Ships were ashore, and two others (ours one of them) got aground on weighing anchor. This will give you some idea of the difficulties we had to encounter. Our ship I have not yet been able to leave but fear it is by far the heaviest sustained in any action during the war, the numbers that were engaged, being considered. The killed of the Navy I understand is upwards of two thousand, the wounded you may therefore compute.

A Flag of Truce was sent in during the latter part of the action by Lord Nelson who wished to spare further effusion of blood, threatening however that should they fire upon the Boats he might send to sure the objects that had stuck to him, he would instantly set fire to them & let their crew shift for themselves. With these terms they thought proper to comply, this truce still continues, but whether we shall accommodate matters, or make a further attempt, I have no opportunity of judging. So much for news.

I have written to my good Mother (seal) some reason to believe she may be anxious (seal) you have occasion to write to both. I trust, (seal) you will have the goodness to say I am well & merry.

With best respects to Mr. Spottiswood & to Mr. Graves, believe me to be

My dear sir

Your sincerely obed. Servant

Sidney Beckwith

Addressed to:
Andrew Strahan, Esq., MP
New Street
London

The following is the muster list of the men of the Rifle Corps transferred to the *Elephant* for the assault and returned to their previous vessel at the end of hostilities.

Surname	First	Qualities	No.	Age Born	Entered	Appeared	Previous
AGNEW	Sergt.	265			31/03/01	31/03/01	London
BALL	William	272			31/03/01	31/03/01	London
BELL	Michael	323			31/03/01	31/03/01	London
BECKWITH	Captain	262			31/03/01	31/03/01	London
BIGGARD	John	273			31/03/01	31/03/01	London
BOOTH	Willliam	261			30/03/01	31/03/01	London
BRADFORD	Corpl.	268			31/03/01	31/0301	London
COX	Corpl.	269			31/03/01	31/03/01	London
COX	John	274			26/03/01	26/03/01	London
CRILLING	Nethias.	275			30/03/01	30/03/01	London

Surname	First	Qualities	No.	Age Born	Entered	Appeared	Previous
CROOKS	John		276		31/03/01	31/03/01	London
DEMPSTER	Geo.		278		31/03/01	31/03/01	London
DILGIE	William		277		31/03/01	31/03/01	London
DOYLE J.	Aidecamp		357		26/03/01	26/03/01	London
DUNNASIA	Thos.		279		31/03/01	31/03/01	London
DUNN	Paul		271		31/03/01	31/03/01	London
FERGUSON	Doctor	Surgeon	264		31/03/01	31/03/01	London
FRAZER	?icker		280		31/03/01	31/03/01	London
GOATTAM	Thos.		282		31/03/01	31/03/01	London
GODFREY	Rich.		281		31/03/01	31/03/01	London
GRAHAM	John	Servnt	258		26/03/01	26/03/01	London
GRANT	James		284		31/03/01	31/03/01	London

Surname	First	Qualities	No.	Age	Born	Entered	Appeared	Previous
GRAY	Dav.	283				31/03/01	31/03/01	London
GRIGG	James	285				31/03/01	31/03/01	London
HALL	Thos.	286				31/03/01	31/03/01	London
HEMMINGS	Phillip	287				31/03/01	31/03/01	London
HEEPTON	Anthony	290				31/03/01	31/03/01	London
HEWETSON	Alex.	289				31/03/01	31/03/01	London
HISLOP	John	288				31/03/01	31/03/01	London
JACKS	James	291				31/03/01	31/03/01	London
KINNEAR	Thos.	293				31/03/01	31/03/01	London
McLEN	James	296				31/03/01	31/03/01	London
McSHRIVER (illegible)	James	298				31/03/01	31/03/01	London

Surname	First	Qualities	No.	Age Born	Entered	Appeared	Previous
MACKINTOSH	Alex.	260			26/03/01	26/03/01	London
MANSER	Alex.	295			31/03/01	31/03/01	London
MARRIN	John	297			31/03/01	31/03/01	London
MARRING	James	302			31/03/01	31/03/01	London
MINTO	John	299			31/03/01	31/03/01	London
MILLS	Saml.	300			31/03/01	31/03/01	London
MITCHELL	Geo	301			31/03/01	31/03/01	London
NEWTON	James	304			31/03/01	31/03/01	London
NICOLLS	George	303			31/03/01	31/03/01	London
PHILLIPS	Willm.	305			31/03/01	31/03/01	London
RAULSTON	James	307			31/03/01	31/03/01	London
SAMPLE	Thomas	316			31/03/01	31/03/01	London

Surname	First	Qualities	No.	Age Born	Entered	Appeared	Previous
SHEPPARD	James		308		31103/01	31/03/31	London
SINNER	George		309		31/03/01	31/03/01	London
SMITH	James		322		31/03/01	31/03/01	London
SMITH	John		310		31/03/01	31/03/01	London
STEEL	Peter		311		31/03/01	31/03/01	London
STOREY	Robt.		318		31/03/01	31/03/01	London
STUART(sic)	Lieut. Col.		356		26/03/01	26/03/31	London
SUTHERLAND	Donald		312		31/03/01	31/03/01	London
TRUO	William		317		31/03/01	31/03/01	London
TURNER	Henry		319		31/03/01	31/03/01	London
TYLER	Alex.		314		31/03/01	31/03/01	London
WALSH	Camise		320		31/03/01	31/03/01	London

Surname	First	Qualities	No.	Age Born	Entered	Appeared	Previous
WHITEARM	Willm.	270			31/03/01	31/03/01	London
WILSON	George	321			31/03/01	31/03/01	London
WOTTEN	Sergt.	267			31/03/01	31/03/01	London

The official report of casualties noted the death of Captain Bawden, a volunteer with the Cornish Rifles, but he was not spotted on the muster list of the *Elephant* and perhaps transferred from another vessel after the commencement of hostilities.

A 74 gun ship of the line, 15 of which were were present at Copenhagen as part of Sir Hyde Parker's battle fleet. These versatile fighting ships emerged from the experience and knowledge gained in ship design towards the end of the eighteenth century. Highly manoeuvrable and fast, but still powerful enough to still stand in line of battle. A firm favourite with both the Admiralty and the sailors who sailed and fought in them. The backbone of the Royal Navy in the Napoleonic period.

HMS *ELEPHANT*

Warships of the Nelson era were a compromise between the weight of armament that could be carried and the fastest speed. The variables in performance, even of ships built to the same design, were a test of the master who had to account for the changes brought about by the age of the vessel, the condition of the hull, the experience of his crew and the vagaries of the wind. Most desirable was the vessel which could hold the weather gauge and get to the windward of the enemy during an encounter. Oak was the favoured timber but the demands of the period scoured much of the available wood from the vicinity of the shipbuilders; aggravated by the demands for fuel for the burgeoning industrial development. Our appreciation of the warships of the period is perhaps romantic, being influenced by *Victory,* at Portsmouth, now being steadily and studiously restored in accordance with the most recent research. Appearing glorious and stilled in her present isolation she would have been a hive of activity and the focus of the relentless movement of men and materials. The reality of crewing a sail-of-the-line during the period was less romantic – they were damp, insanitary and overcrowded – smelling of tar, bilge-water, sodden timber, old salt-meat, rum, gunpowder and particularly of closely packed bodies. On blockade and searching for the enemy before Trafalgar, Nelson spent almost two years at sea without setting foot on land. His friend Collingwood similarly kept at sea on one occasion for twenty two months without dropping anchor, and indeed finally died in harness through his commitment to duty. It was not a life for the fainthearted but the threat of republicanism meant that many seamen were coerced to their duty.

Classification and Rating

The rating of ships refers to the number of guns carried. A **first rate** carried from 100 to 110 guns upwards; a **second rate** carries from 84 to 98; a **third rate** 64 to 84; **fourth rate** 40 to 50; **fifth rate** 28 to 38 and **sixth rates**, any number of guns up to 24 if commanded by a post-captain. (the number of the guns did vary over time). Only ships of the first three rates were considered as ships-of-the-line, able through their armament, to be powerful enough to lie in the line of battle.

H.M.S. Elephant

Sir Thomas Slade was surveyor to the Navy Board from 1755 to 1771., and considered the most successful British warship designer – responsible for a series of very successful three-deckers, two-deckers, frigates and smaller craft including the classic *HMS Victory*. During his period *HMS Elephant* , a third rate 74, was built from the Group known as Arrogant Class 1758, which included Nelson's flagship at the Nile – *HMS Vanguard.* The *Elephant* carried the following armament:- Gundeck 28 x 32 pounders Upper Deck 28 x 18 pdrs. Quarter Deck 14 x 32 pdr carronades Forecastle 2 x 9 pdrs plus 2 x 32 pdr carronades.

Contract to build the vessel

The cover of the contract to build the vessel (NMM) is endorsed ' Contract with Mr George Parsons for the building of a 74 Gunship named 'The Elephant'', and contains 25 pages of detailed printed instruction regarding the structure of the vessel.

The document is endorsed that it was contracted and agreed on the twenty sixth day of December 1781.

Amongst the detail is the following:-

'LENGTHS	Keel 138 feet 3 3/8inches	Gundeck 168 feet 0 inches.
BURTHEN IN TONS	1604	
DRAUGHT	Afore 20 feet 4 inches	Abaft 21 feet 10 inches

TIMBER and PLANK That all the Timber and Plank shall be of the growth of **England**, except the Plank of the Bottom under the light Draught of Water, which may be **East Country** Plank, provided it be good white Crown Plank, otherwise to the English Plank, all the Crutches, Knees, Standards, Riders and Breast Hooks to have so full a Faying of Spine against the respective Beams, Sides, Decks, and Ceiling, that the Bolts of Fastning of each may not be naked when the Sap rots away, as has too frequently appeared to the evident weakning of those Ships formerly built in Merchants Yards, and has proved the principal Means of their too soon decay; and also the whole Frame to be well grown, square edged, free from Sap, Shakes or Defects, and that that all the Plank of the Bottom, Sides and Decks, shall be dry and well seasoned before it is wrought, and that the **Prussian** Deals for the Decks, &c. be good yellow Wood, free from Sap, Shakes or Defects, and that no Sap shall be wrought in the Edges of them.

IRON-WORK All the Iron-work shall be wrought of the best tough **Swedish** Iron, not burnt or hurt in working; all the Bolts to be clenched or belayed, as shall be directed by the Officers or Overseer inspecting the said Works. Those to the Iron Knees and Standards to be drove through them into the Transoms, Beams, or Timbers, and all clenched on Rings let into the Wood.

TREENAILS All the Tree-Nails to be dry, seasoned, clear of Sap, and converted from Timbers of the growth of **Sussex**, or equal in goodness thereto, to be well mooted, not over hauled with an Axe in driving, and all to be well caulked and wedged at both Ends.

TIME OF LAUNCHING The following entry is handwritten on the contract against the marginal heading '*And I do oblige myself that all the works of the said ship shall be performed and perfected as beforementioned agreeable to the Draught or Draughts that accompany this contract, launched and put safe into the hands of such Officer or Officers as shall be appointed to receive her by or before the expiration of Forty five calendar months from the signing hereof; But in case of the said Commissioners should think proper that the said ship should stand to season, it is agreed that whatever time she shall so stand to season is to be allowed the contract of in addition to the time before mentioned for completing her.....*'

The record shows that the vessel was launched by Parsons, Bursledon on the Hamble 24.8.1786
Hand written entries on the plan for building the ship also note:- '*Goliath Vanguard Excellent* @ Harwich *Saturn* @ Northam *Elephant* @ Burlesdon *Illustrious* ' Bucklers Hard *Bellerophon* @ Medway *Zealous* @ Deptford *Audacious* @ Thames'
She was subsequently reduced to 58 guns 4th rate, and finally broken up 11/1830

Figurehead

The figurehead for the *Elephant* was carved by the Hellyer Family of ship carvers to the Navy   Records show that the carvers sent a price for the bow carving of £16 to the Navy but this was cut down by the Navy Board to £11! (information courtesy of Richard Hunter, Figurehead Historian).   Enquiries to date have not identified the detail of the figurehead but it is reasonable to anticipate it would include some representation of an elephant.   By coincidence, in the Road giving access to the harbour, the Danes had placed their *Elephanten* blockship whose figurehead included the head of an elephant.

Draught

Nelson transferred from the *St. George* to conduct the assault on Copenhagen and some indication of the difference between the vessels may be gained by reference to the 'Establishment'.   The *St. George* was a 3 decker carrying 750 men and 90 guns; the *Elephant* a 2 decker, carrying 550 men and 70 guns with a difference in draught between the vessels of about 17 inches.   The difference may appear marginal but it is clear from the groundings, which occurred during the attack and the withdrawal, that Nelson was wise to transfer his flag.

Masters logs – *St. George* and *Elephant*

A master was appointed after examination by 'one of the senior captains and three of the best qualified masters'.   He was responsible for the 'conduct of the ship from port to port' under the direction of the captain, kept the official logbook, and was highly respected.   He controlled the sailing of the ship, the trimming and settings of her sails, and the guidance of her movements during a battle.   He was key to all the activities of a successful ship and amongst his duties, which enable us to gain a glimpse into the formalities of his life, was the supervision of the writing of the log book by his mates.   Entries included details of the weather, ship's position, expenditure of stores, and daily happenings, etc., from the reports and records of the ship's officers.   Extracts covering the period of the conflict are noted in the following abstracts from the logs of Nelson's flagship on route to Copenhagen, *St. George*, and the *Elephant* to which he transferred his flag for the assault due to it's shallower draught.

Sailors raising the anchor by capstan
(from an old print)

ADM 52/ 3399 Master's log *HMS St. George*.

The endorsement on the front cover of the Master's Log contains the following certificate: -

'Admiralty Office 21 Aug 1802

These are to certify that *Mr Thos. Atkinson Master of* His Majesty's *Ship* the *St. George* having satisfied my Lords Commissioners of the Admiralty that between the *11th February 1801* and the *27 July 1802* the said ship was not in any place where he had an opportunity of useful observations or Coasts, Roads, & Co. their Lordships have not objection to the Payment of the Wages due to him for the said time, on account of his not having given such observations to this office.

Signed Evan Nepean'

The log includes the following entries: -

'February 1801	HM Ship St. George moored in Torbay 1801
Wednesday 11th	Moderate breezes from the ESE – Cloudy weather. Hoisted Vice Admiral Lord Nelson's Flag on board – Admiral the Earl St. Vincent flag being hosted on board the San Josef from HM Ship Ville de Paris. Joined the ship Vice Admiral Lord Nelson, Thos. Masterman Hardy, Esq., Capt. AM Strong breezes from the NE cloudy and rather a heavy swell from the ESE
Thursday 12th	Admiral Earl St. Vincent struck his flag San Josef. Sent cutter to Brixham for fresh beef.
21 March 1801	Fresh gales and snow @ intervals
29 miles distance	Osprey brig made signal to the admiral having gained soundings in 5 fm she then bore
of log. Water	SSE from the St George's quarter deck dist. 4? Miles when other soundings at that time
expended 5 butts	Was 28 fms. And the town Warberg bore (position against town and compass bearing difficult
Remains 264 ton	to interpret) Anholt Island. The soundings did not alter 2 feet during the different bearings of the
Served Grog	lighthouse and the island of Anholt.
	Latitude observation 56:36N

30 March 1801	0800 Firing commenced from Cronenburgh Castle @ the van Division
31 March 1801	HMS Amazon reconnoitring the fortifications and junks ships in Copenhagen who opened very heavy fire of shells and great guns at her Departed this life Patrick Wilson Lieuts. Pearce and Layman left the ship with two flat bottom boats having the Rifle Corps party To go to the Isis Employed scraping the ships side for painting
1 April 1801	Employed painting the larboard
2 April 1801	Action commenced on the Van Division abreast Copenhagen Kings Ground 10.30 Edgar commenced 10.40 London 10.50 Ardent 11.15 Elephant

The Master's 'Remarks' covering the period of the event is also of interest, as it routinely records duties aboard the vessel and the activity leading directly to the opening of hostilities:

'Remarks for Thursday 2nd April 1801

0100hrs Moderate breezes and Cloudy weather. Empl. As necessary about the Rigging.
At 3:30 Van Division weighed and made sail into the South Channel of the Grounds.
At 4:40 Van Division all anchored.
0700hrs Light Breezes and Cloudy Weather
0900hrs Do Breezes and Weather
1100hrs Do Breezes and Weather
0100hrs Sent all the Boats & Launch with the S?hearm Cable Manned and Armed to the Van Division
At 9:30 weighed and made all sail on the Larboard Tack. Tacked ship occasionally.

Remarks for Thursday 2nd April 1801 continued:-

At 10:25 action commenced on the Van Division abreast of Copenhagen Kings Ground.
At 10:30 London 94 Ramilies and Veteran
At 10:35 Firing seen from the Junk Ships
At 10:38 Edgar commenced firing on the enemy.
At 10:40 London 112 General
At 10:50 Ardent began firing
At 11:15 Elephant 16 General to the Van Division
At 11:56 London 34
At 11:57 London 66 Agamemnon
At 11:59 Elephant 34 Van Division.
Tacked ship occasionally

At Noon Copenhagen SWbS Dist. 7 miles.
London South ½ miles Van Division and the enemy still engaging……………
No observation Water expended 5 Butts – Remains 235 Tons

Remarks Friday 3rd April 1801
0100hrs Moderate Breezes and Cloud.
At 0:30 **London 39 General** with 2 Guns. Engagement still continuing – Tacked ship occasionally.
At 2:10 London 63 Amazon.
At 2:20 London 63 Ramilies.
At 2:25 Annulled the Ramilies Signal.
At 2:45 London 91 to the Elephant, Raisonable and Defence.

Remarks Friday 3rd April 1801 continued:-

At 3 London 63 General.
At 3:5 A Flag of Truce came from Copenhagen to the Elephant.
At 3:10 London 191 Centre Division.
At 2:25 Elephant 63 Isis. At 3:26 firing ceased on both sides.
At 3:30 London 191 Ramilies.
At 3:40 Defiance 3 & 4 to the London.
At 3:50 Monarch 3 & 4 to the London.
At 4:10 one of the Enemy's two decks blew up.
At 4:50 shortened sail & came too with the Best Bower Anchor in 7 fathoms in Copenhagen Roads
and veered the half cable Service – all the Centre Division at Anchor –
When at anchor Mole Head of Copenhagen Dist 3 miles.
At 5:15 London hoisted the Truce Flag.
Enemys Vessels taken The Prevesteen 64, Holstein 64, Infosbutten 64, Vogerin 50, Jutland 64,
Charlotte Amelia 26, Cronenburgh 26, Shark 24, Rensborg 24, Sea Horse 20 and Speirfish 18, Zealand 74
Moderate Breezes and Cloudy weather Employed as necessary.
At Noon Moderate Breezes and Cloudy weather Water expended 5 butts Remains 232 ½ tons Served Grog'

In the margin of the narrative entry it shows the wind as:-South at 0100hrs SW at 1400hrs and by 2400 hrs NW. The vagaries of the wind are clear from the foregoing entry and show how fortunate Nelson had been as his squadron skirted the Middle Ground with a southerly wind and enjoyed a northerly breeze to move into the assault.

The following entries in the log are brief and the page is headed:-

'His Majesty's Ship St. George at Anchor in Copenhagen Roads 1801'

Friday 3rd April 1801	Light breezes from the WSW to N and Cloudy Weather Employed as necessary about the Rigging. At Sunset hoisted Lord Nelson's Flag. The Flat Boats and Rifle Corps returned From the Isis
Saturday 4th April	AM ditto Breezes and Weather. Sent Fifty men to the Assistance of HMS Defiance – Carpenters crew to the assistance of the Elephant and Monarch. Water expended 5 Butts Remains 230 Tons Served Grog
Sunday 5th April	Light Breezes from the SSW and Clear Weather. Employed as necessary.. Sailmakers repairing the Elephant's Tops. Sent a party of men on board the Danish Prize ship Holstein. AM ditto Breezes and weather. Empd. As necessary assisting the Defiance, Elephant, Monarch and Prize ship Holstein. Departed this Life John Cornele Seaman. Fresh breezes at NW and rain with snow at intervals Water expended 5 Butts Remains 227 ½ Tons. Served Grog
Monday 6th April	Moderate breezes at WSW and Cloud Weather with rain at intervals. Burnt Two of the Prize Ships of War. Recd. On board 155 prisoners. AM Fresh breezes at WNW and Cloudy Weather. Employed repairing the Elephant's sails and fitting the Holstein Prize Came off the Flag of Truce from Copenhagen Water Expended 5 Butts. Remains 225 Tons. Served Grog.

Tuesday 7th April	Fresh Breezes from the NW to SW and Cloudy weather. Employed as necessary about the rigging and fitting the Holstein prize. AM ditto Breezes and weather – Burnt two of the Prize ships of war. Came off a Flag of Truce from Copenhagen. Water expended 5 Butts Remains 222 ½ Tons Served Grog
Wednesday 8th April	Fresh breezes from the SW and Cloudy weather Sent Lieut. Elliot with 50 men on board the Holstein prize ship to fit her. Employed as necessary repairing sails for the squadron. AM Moderate breezes from the SbW & drizzling rain. Empd. As necessary. At 10 London 214 Centre Division and Signal for Petty Officers. Water expended 6 Butts Remains 219 ½ Tons Served Grog.
Thursday 9th April	Moderate Breezes from the South and drizzling rain. Employed as necessary about the Rigging. AM Moderate Breezes from the NW & Cloudy Weather Employed fitting the Holstein prize. Loosed sails to dry. Water expended 5 Butts Remains 217 Tons Served Grog.
Friday 10th April	Moderate Breezes from the NW & Cloudy weather. Employed fitting the Holstein prize. Arrived here the Drathe? cutter and Rover Lugger from England. London hauled down the Flag of Truce. AM Moderate breezes from the SSW And Cloudy weather. Came out of Copenhagen 4 Danish Sloops for the Danish Prisoners. At 8 London Genl. For Lieutenants. Set the Zealand of 74 guns prize ship on Fire. At noon fresh breezes & cloudy veered to the whole cable ???? Water expended 5 Butts Remains 214 ½ tons Served Grog.

ADM 52/ 2968 Master's log HMS Elephant

The cover for the Master's Log includes the endorsement:
'A journal of the proceedings on board HM Ship Elephant, Thos. Foley, Esq., Commander commencing the 26th day of March 1801, and ending the 31st day of August 1801.'

Below are some entries of interest from the log:- March 1801 Friday 27th
At 01pm Vice Admiral Lord Nelson shifted his flag from the St. George to this ship

At anchor in the mouth Of The Sound	AM moderate and fair washed the ship Employed variously – made signal for several captains. Repeated the signal to exercise the great guns & small arms
March 1801 Mon 30th in the road of Copenhagen	Made sail past Cronberg Castle – Danes opened a heavy fire without effect And our bombs commence fire. Lord Nelson went on board the Amazon to reconnoitre the enemy having the ??? brig and lugger to attend
April 1 At anchor The outer road of Copenhagen	Employed variously – shifted the stern cable to the starboard side
April 2 Thurs At Anchor bet The town of Copen-hagen and Middle Ground	Moderate breezes and fair. At 3pm weighed with the van division, frigates bombs and ran through the passage between the Middleground and Flathom At 5 anchored in 6 fathoms.....the Edgar weighed and led the squadron to the attack of the Danish line as per margin and moored on the bank of Copenhagen the ships of squadron followed in succession and anchored opposite the enemy and fired as they Arrived at their stations which commenced about ½ past 10am

AFTERMATH

On the *St. George* Nelson's hectic day concluded with brief notes to Emma and his journal entry, which read: -

'Moderate breeze southerly at ½ past nine made the signal to weigh and to engage the Danish line. The action began at 5 minutes past ten and lasted about four hours, when 17 out of 18 of the Danish line were taken burnt or sunk. Our ships suffered a good deal. At night went on board the St. George, very unwell.'

The fragile peace was disturbed in the early hours of the following morning, by shot from a Danish vessel, prompting a note from Nelson to his commander in chief written at 3am! With the pragmatism, which marked the British Navy of the period, work had commenced immediately upon the cessation of gunfire to seek to repair the damaged vessels, so far as circumstances allowed; though some had finally to limp home. Despite a disturbed night Nelson rose early and, with Hardy, visited the *Elephant,* which had floated off the shoals, and toured the Danish prizes.

On the 3rd April 1801 Nelson reported formally to his commander-in-chief as follows:-

TO VICE-ADMIRAL SIR HYDE PARKER

Sir, In obedience to your directions to report the proceedings of the Squadron named in the margin, which you did me the honour to place under my command, I beg leave to inform you, that having, by the assistance of that able Officer, Captain Riou, and the unremitting exertions of Captain Brisbane, and the Masters of the Amazon and the Cruizer in particular, buoyed the Channel of the Outer Deep, and the position of the Middle Ground, the Squadron passed in safety, and anchored off Draco the evening of the 1st; and that yesterday morning I made the signal for the Squadron to weigh, and to engage the Danish Line, consisting of six Sail of the Line, eleven Floating Batteries, mounting from twenty-six twenty-four pounders to eighteen eighteen-pounders, and one Bomb-Ship, besides Schooner Gun-Vessels. These were supported by the Crown Islands, mounting eighty-eight cannon, and four Sail of the Line, moored in the Harbour's Mouth and some Batteries on the Island of Amak.

The Bomb-Ship and Schooner Gun-Vessels made their escape. The other seventeen Sail are sunk, burnt, or taken, being the whole of the Danish Line to the southward of the Crown Islands, after a battle of four hours.

From the very intricate navigation, the Bellona and Russell unfortunately grounded, but although.not in the situation assigned them yet so placed as to be of great service. The Agamemnon could not weather the shoal of the middle, and was obliged to anchor, but not the smallest blame can be attached to Captain Fancourt: it was an event to which all the Ships were liable. These accidents prevented the extension of our Line by the three Ships before mentioned, who would, I am confident, have silenced the Crown Islands, the two outer Ships in the harbour's mouth, and prevented the heavy loss in the Defiance and Monarch; and which unhappily threw the gallant and good Captain Riou, (to whom I had given command of the Frigates and Sloops named in the margin, to assist in the attack of the Ships at the harbour's mouth) under a very heavy fire. The consequence has been the death of Captain Riou, and many brave Officers and men in the Frigates and Sloops.

The Bombs were directed and took their stations abreast of the Elephant, and threw some shells into the Arsenal. Captain Rose, who volunteered his services to direct the Gun-brigs, did everything that was possible to get them forward, but the current was too strong for them to be of service during the Action; but not the less merit is due to Captain Rose, and, I believe, all the Officers and crews of the Gun-Brigs, for their exertions.

The Boats of those Ships of the Fleet who were not ordered on the attack, afforded us every assistance; and the Officers and men who were in them merit my warmest approbation. The *Desirée* took her station in raking the southernmost Danish Ship of the Line, and performed the greatest service. The Action began at five minutes past ten – the Van led by Captain George Murray of the *Edgar*, who set a noble example of intrepidity, which was as well followed up by every Captain, Officer, and Man in the Squadron.

It is my duty to state to you the high and distinguished merit and gallantry of Rear-Admiral Graves. To Captain Foley, who permitted me the honour of hoisting my Flag in the *Elephant*, I feel under the greatest obligations; his advice was necessary on many and important occasions during the battle. I beg leave to express how much I feel indebted to every

Captain, Officer, and Man, for their zeal and distinguished bravery on this occasion. The Honourable Colonel Steward did me the favour to be on board the *Elephant*; and himself, with every Officer and Soldier under his orders, shared with pleasure the toils and dangers of the day.
The loss in such a Battle has naturally been very heavy. Amongst many other brave Officers and men who were killed, I have with sorrow to place the name of Captain Mosse, of the Monarch, who has left a wife and six children to lament his loss; and among the wounded, that of Captain Sir Thomas Boulden Thompson, of the *Bellona*. I have the honour to be, & c.,
NELSON AND BRONTE.

[Marginal note: *Elephant, Defiance, Monarch, Bellona, Edgar, Russell, Ganges, Glatton, Isis, Agamemnon, Polyphemus, Ardent;* [Frigates] *Amazon, Desirée, Blanche, Alcmene*; Sloops – *Dart, Arrow, Cruizer, and Harpy*; Fire-Ships –*Zephyr and Otter.* Bombs – *Discovery, Sulphur, Hecla, Explosion, Zebra, Terror and Volcano*]

Nelson took his report to the *London* and was advised the Danish Parliament would not leave the Armed Neutrality but had verbally offered to mediate between the parties if Britain lifted the embargo – leaving matters as uncertain as before the engagement. Admiral Sir Hyde Parker directed Nelson to attend on the Crown Prince to seek a formal agreement to end hostilities. Landing by barge, accompanied by Hardy and Captain Thesiger, as interpreter, Nelson and his party were offered a carriage, but walked through crowds to the Amalienborg Palace. (Hardy later commented they were acclaimed as at 'The Lord Mayor's Show'). Arriving at noon the party dined before Nelson and the Crown Prince talked for two hours. The discussions were polite, but on Nelson's part brusque, as he sought to press the issue. From Nelson:- 'In speaking of the pretended union of the Northern Powers, I could not help saying that his Royal Highness must be sensible that it was nonsense to talk of a mutual protection of trade with a power that had none, and that he must be sensible that the Emperor of Russia would never have thought of offering to protect the trade of Denmark if he had not had hostility against Great Britain'. Finally Nelson returned to the fleet but did not think the Danes would withdraw from the Armed Neutrality nor accept the British Fleet's presence in the Baltic – for fear of Russia. The period of truce was extended as the Danes wrestled with their fears for the future and Nelson pressed the Crown Prince to either join with the British or disarm. Further letters were exchanged before finally the Armistice was signed, by Nelson and Colonel Stewart on behalf of Britain, and later ratified by Parker.

Writing to the Prime Minister Addington later the same day Nelson noted :-

'1st We had beat the Danes;

2nd We wish to make them feel that we are their real friends, therefore have spared their Town, which we can always set on fire; and I do not think if we burnt Copenhagen it would have the effect of attaching them to us; on the contrary they would hate us.

3rd They understand perfectly that we are at war with them for their treaty of Armed Neutrality made last year.

4th We have made them suspend the operations of that treaty.

5th It has given our Fleet free scope to act against Russia and Sweden;

6th Which we never should have done, although Copenhagen would have been burnt, for Sir Hyde was determined not to have Denmark hostile in his rear. Our passage over the Grounds might have been very seriously interrupted by the batteries near Draco.

7th Every reinforcement, even a cutter, can join us without molestation, and also provisions, stores &c.

8th Great Britain is left with the stake of all the Danish property in her hands, he colonies, &c., if she refuses peace.

9th The hands of Denmark are tied up; ours are free to act against her confederate allies.

10th Although we might have burnt the City, I have my doubts whether we could their ships.'

With the end of hostilities Nelson sought to persuade Sir Hyde to sail for Revel to attack the Russian vessels held there by the ice but his Commander-in-Chief declined. To the further disgust of Nelson, and much of the fleet, Sir Hyde had ordered the destruction of the Danish prizes thereby denying the sailors the rare opportunity of prize money. Further frustration was caused with the promotions by Sir Hyde from the *London* to fill the vacancies caused by the fatalities in the battle. Men who had acquitted themselves bravely under fire with Nelson were passed over to suit the favourites of the Commander-in-Chief who had merely observed the conflict.

As ever, once the adrenalin of action ceased, Nelson's letters to his friends and to Emma revealed the melancholy side to his nature. He was desperate to return home to see Emma and their daughter, and in one letter reflected that a year earlier, they had cruised the Mediterranean in happier circumstances. The introspection was short lived as Nelson received a note from Sir Hyde reporting the Swedish Fleet at sea and asking that he join the *Elephant*! Nelson's reaction was seen by the master of the *Edgar* who happened to be present, and he commented that his immediate response was to summon a boat to be manned which he boarded immediately without waiting for a boat cloak despite the prospect of 24 mile row against the wind and current. 'All I had ever seen or heard of him could not half so clearly prove to me the singular and unbounded zeal of this truly great man. His anxiety in the boat for nearly six hours (lest the Fleet should have sailed before he got on board one of them, and lest we should not catch the Swedish squadron) is beyond all conception. I will quote some expressions in his own words. It was extremely cold, and I wished him to put on a great coat of mine that was in the boat: 'No, I am not cold; my anxiety for my Country will keep me warm. Do you think the Fleet has sailed?' 'I should suppose not, my Lord.' 'If they are, we shall follow them to Carlskrona by the boat, by God!' I merely state this to show how his thoughts must have been employed. The idea of going in a small boat, rowing six oars, without a single morsel of anything to drink, the distance of about 150 miles must convince the world that every other earthly consideration than that of serving his country was totally banished from his thoughts.' It turned out to be a false alarm and, in a note to Troubridge, Nelson acknowledged his thanks to Sir Hyde 'for to have been left behind in the expectation of an action would have been worse than death'. He also commented that he hoped the next despatches from England would bring his leave of absence but, despite his pleas to be allowed to return, Sir Hyde it was who was finally summoned to return with Nelson appointed in his stead. Sir Hyde transferred to the *Blanche* for his return to England and Nelson hastily wrote a number of formal and personal letters, taking advantage of the returning vessel. His immediate action thereafter was to signal for the fleet to prepare to sail for the Baltic! Together with the summons for the return of Sir Hyde Parker, information had been received of the death of Czar Paul with the possibility of an improved relationship with Russia. Nonetheless Nelson took a pragmatic line in his approach to the Russian representatives at Revel which prompted a curt exchange of notes before matters were amicably settled, releasing British merchant shipping, and resulting in a personal invitation for Lord Nelson to attend Petersburg.

Nelson was made a viscount and Rear-Admiral Graves received a knighthood. In a ceremony on board the *St. George* on 14 June 1801 Sir Thomas Graves was invested as a Knight of the Most Honourable Order of the Bath. Finally on 19 June Nelson sailed for England, to Emma and their daughter Horatia. On arrival at Yarmouth he first visited the Naval Hospital and toured the wards with a Doctor, visiting all sailors wounded in action. The doctor recorded one of the exchanges:-

> Nelson: "Well, Jack what's the matter with you?" Sailor: "Lost my arm, your honour."
>
> Nelson: [glancing down at his empty sleeve before turning again to the sailor] "Well, Jack then you and I are forever spoiled for fishermen; cheer up, my brave fellow."

Returning to London Nelson immediately sought to render assistance and support to Sir Hyde who, smarting at his recall, sought an Inquiry into his conduct in the Baltic. His letters to Sir Hyde were wise and solicitous on behalf of his former commander who was thanked by parliament but not reappointed.

In 1807 Denmark were again considered to be acting against British interests, being associated with France and influencing trade through the Baltic. Lord Gambier first invested then bombarded Copenhagen for three days. Considerable damage was done and fires started which grew so serious that the commandant agreed to a cease-fire. All the seaworthy ships of the Danish Navy were then taken to England. Despite the death of Nelson in 1805 at the battle of Trafalgar folklore continues to attribute this incident to his name. The *St. George* continued a presence in the Baltic over the years and sadly was lost together with the *Hero* and *Defence* and a total of 1300 lives off the coast of Denmark on Christmas Eve 1811 as they left the area before the weather imprisoned the vessels in ice.

COPENHAGEN MEDALS

Nelson, no less than Jervis, cared deeply for the interests of officers and seamen who had shared battle with him. He fought for their rights and honours; and never so tenaciously, albeit unsuccessfully, as against the absence of medals for the victory at Copenhagen on 2 April 1801. Nelson began his campaign just three days after the battle when he wrote this general comment to Jervis, '....believe me, I have weighed all circumstances, and my conscience I think the King should send a gracious message to the House of Commons, for a gift to this Fleet....I shall leave it to the better judgement of your Lordship and Mr. Addington...'. (Admiralty Lord). Later, he was more specific, '....and I long to have a Medal which I would not give up to be made an English Duke....'.

After a seven months wait (20 Nov., 1801), Nelson, not without a justified impatience, took the opportunity to further the case. He wrote three letters, one each to :

- the **Lord Mayor** after the City of London had voted its thanks, pleading on behalf of '....the brave fellows, my companions in danger that I have not failed, at every proper place, to represent... their bravery and meritorious services....'. The Lord Mayor promised only to '....give the subject a proper and early consideration'. Nelson had to withdraw this letter.

The following year, London tried again to offer its thanks to Nelson for other services. Nelson declined, refused to dine with the Lord Mayor and characteristically declared he '....would never wear his other medals till that for Copenhagen was granted'.

- **Addington**, forwarding too a copy of his letter to the Lord Mayor a few days later. In his letter to Addington, he again made his request and added, '....Lord St. Vincent, in July made me truly happy to the assurance that the King would grant medals to those who fought that day, as has been usual in other great naval victories.....'.

Addington replied by expressing anxiety '....that on the subject in question, no letter, be the terms of it what they may, be written by your Lordship to the Lord Mayor. It could be productive of no good, and might, and (I firmly believe) would lead to serious embarrassment...'. Nelson thus withdrew his letter to the Lord Mayor.

- **Jervis**, again enclosing a copy of his letter to the Lord Mayor, adding '....Your Lordship's opinion of the services of that day induced you to hold out hopes amounting to certainty. I believed that the King would grant those who fought that day, Medals, as has been done for other great victories, and I have been, I own, expecting them daily since the King's return from Weymouth.....'.
Jervis replied with two letters, both dated the day after. The first acknowledged the copy of the Lord Mayor's letter. The second was a devastating blow, '....I must beg leave to assure you that I have given no encouragement to the other subject therein mentioned, but , on the contrary, have explained to your Lordship, and to Mr. Addington, the impropriety of such a measure being recommended to the King....'.
In emotional shock, Nelson replied the following day, '....I was thunderstruck by the reading of your Lordship'' letter, telling me that you had never given me encouragement to the expectation of receiving Medals for the Action of April 2. Had I so understood you, I never should, the same day, have told Mr. Addington how happy you made me, by the assurance that the King would give us medals; and I have never failed assuring the Captains, that I have seen and communicated with, that they might depend on receiving them. I own I considered the words your Lordship used as conveying assurance. It was an apology for their not being given before, which, I understood you, they would have been, but for the difficulty of fixing who was to have them; and, I trust you will recollect that my reply was that 'certainly they could not be given to any but those who fought'; I could not., have had any interest in misunder-standing you.... I must beg that your Lordship reconsider your conversation... and think that I could not but believe that we were to have the medals.... I am truly made ill by your letter. If any person had told me what your wrote, I would have staked my head against the assertion....'. To which Jervis replied the next day, '....That you have perfectly mistaken all that passed between us in the conversation you allude to, is most certainly and I cannot possibly depart from the opinion I gave your Lordship in my last....'.
Nelson summarized it bitterly to Alexander Davison, '....Either Lord St. Vincent or myself are liars: so my affairs stand...'
Nelson had a final meeting with Addington in December 1801 spoke his mind and got nowhere. To Captain Sutton (Amazon) he repeated his complaint: 'I have been so much engaged and hurried about no notice being taken by the City

of London of our April 2nd. And by Lord St. Vincent who, in contradiction to what I thought was a most positive assurance that we were to have Medals, now tells me, that he has always thought it improper to recommend it to the King....'. adding later, '....Lord St. Vincent's conduct about the Medals of Copenhagen, appears to me extraordinary....'.

Nelson and his Captains never gave up. In 1804 when Melville succeeded Jervis as First Lord, Nelson wrote forcefully to him reiterating his claim and enclosed the Jervis correspondence. He received his first forthright answer why, three years after the battle, the Government felt it expedient to refuse:...'when Badges of Triumph are bestowed in the heat and conflict of war, they do not rankle in the minds even of the enemy, at whose expense they are bestowed but the feeling, I suspect, would be very different in Denmark, if the present moment was to be chosen for opening afresh wounds...'.

NAVAL GENERAL SERVICE MEDAL

On the 1st of June 1847, by General Order, Queen Victoria commanded that a medal should be struck to recognise, very belatedly, the services of the Navy from 1793 to 1815. This was later extended to 1840. This medal, dated 1848, was distributed the following year. A possible two hundred and thirty clasps to commemorate each major battle, frigate or boat action were issued to be fixed to the medal, the ribbon being white with blue edges.

The great delay in issuing this token of recognition is best illustrated by the medal awarded to a recipient aboard the *Tremendous* for the action of The Glorious 1st of June 1794. A Mrs McKenzie gave birth to a son aboard the *Tremendous* on the day of the battle, the poor child was christened Daniel Tremendous McKenzie. He was fifty-five years of age when at last he received his medal.

In 1849, the medal was issued to all officers and men who were still alive, and a clasp for COPENHAGEN was given, making this clasp the only recognition given by the Crown to the British fleet for one of Nelson's hardest fought and hardest won battles.

ACKNOWLEDGEMENTS

The authors wish to acknowledge the help and co-operation of the following, whose assistance has smoothed the way in the production of this book:

George Caldwell
Sim Comfort
Graham Dean
Peter Goodwin
Derek Hayes

Richard Hunter, Figurehead Historian
The Late Professor Emilio J. Moriconi
National Maritime Museum

Commander Bruce Nicolls OBE., Vexillographer
Robert Grigor Taylor
Anthony Cross, Warwick Leadlay Gallery

BIBLIOGRAPHY

Horatio Nelson	Tom Pocock, Bodley Head
Naval Biographical Dictionary	William R. O'Byrne
Naval Records for Genealogists	NAM Rodgers,
Nelson's Heroes	Graham Dean & Keith Evans The Nelson Society
Nelson The Immortal Memory	David and Stephen Howarth, Dent & Sons Ltd
Nelson's Navy	Brian Lavery, Conway, Maritime Press Ltd
Nelson Dispatch Volume 4 Part 5 page 86	The Nelson Society
Nelson	Carola Oman, Hodder and Stoughton
Oxford Companion to Ships and the Sea	Oxford University Press Editor Peter Kemp
Public Record Office, Kew	
Rifle Green at Waterloo	George Caldwell and Robert Cooper
Sailing Navy List	David Lyon, Conway Maritime Press
The Battle of Copenhagen Roads	Captain F. Volke The Nelson Society
The Great Gamble	Dudley Pope, Weidenfeld and Nicolson
The Nelson Dispatch	The Nelson Society
The Dispatches and Letters of Lord Nelson	Nicolas, Chatham Publishing reprint
The Rifle Brigade History Volumes 1 & 2	Lieut. Col. Willoughby Verner

THE NELSON SOCIETY 2001

Founded 1981 – Registered Charity No. 296979

President
The Right Honourable The Earl Nelson

Life Vice-Presidents
Mrs Anna Tribe, O.B.E. J.P. – Clive Richards O.B.E.

Executive Chairman
Derek HAYES
16 Silver Lane, Billingshurst, W. Sussex RH14 9RJ Tel/Fax 01403 782496 Email: derek.hayes@which.net

Vice Chairman
Victor SHARMAN
Ballinger Grange, Gt. Missenden, Bucks HP16 9LQ Tel/Fax 01494 862691 Email: vicaletti@talk21.com

Email: nelson.society@rjt.co.uk
Websites: www.rjt.co.uk/Nelson/
Topsail group: http://board.to.topsail

The Nelson Dispatch

The purpose of the **Nelson Dispatch** is to further
the aims of **The Nelson Society** which is to promote
public education and appreciation of
the character and life of Admiral Lord Nelson

THE NELSON SOCIETY

LIST OF PUBLICATIONS

1983	Nelson and Associated Heraldry – A Guide***	R.C. Fiske
1984	Santa Cruz***	Michael Nash
1985	Nelson Commemorative Medals 1797-1905	Thomas A Hardy
1987	A catalogue of Picture Postcards	David Shannon
1988	The Men who fought with NELSON in HMS VICTORY at TRAFALGAR***	Charles Addis MBE
1989	A tour along the Norfolk/Suffolk Border in Nelson and Suckling Country***	Michael Nash
	Notices of Nelson extracted from Norfolk and Norwich Notes and Queries	R.C. Fiske
1990	The Battle of Copenhagen Roads	Captain F. Volke
	Invincible 1765-1801	Derek Hayes
1991	A Brief Guide to Nelson and Bath***	Louis Hodgkin
1992	A visit to Melford Hall, home of Sir Richard Hyde Parker, Bt.	Derek Hayes
1994	Nelson's Heroes	Graham Dean and Keith Evans
	Nelson: The Sussex Tradition***	David Shannon
1998	Horatia Nelson Ward 1801-1881 – Factfile	David Shannon
	HMS VANGUARD at the NILE – the men, the ship, the battle	Eric Tushingham John Morewood Derek Hayes

1999	Nelsoniana. An anthology of Notes and Queries from TP's Weekly 1905	David Shannon
	Admiral Nelson & HMS Victory	Peter Green
2000	Nelson's Overland Return in 1800	Thomas Blümel
	Admiral Nelson and Joseph Haydn	Otto Erich Deutsch

Pamphlets

1997	Admiral Lord Nelson	Rona Dickinson
	Collecting Nelson Postcards	David Shannon
	Nelson's Last Walk	Colin White

***Out of print

Copies, including back copies of The Nelson Dispatch and indexes, are available from:
The Sales Manager, 16 Silver Lane, BILLINGSHURST, West Susssex RH14 9RJ.
Tel/Fax: 01403 782496 Email derek.hayes@which.net

REAR COVER ILLUSTRATION

The Naval General Service Medal awarded to Captain Alfred Luckraft (1792-1871).
(The Clifford Mansfield Collection)

Having joined the navy as a First Class volunteer he served in this capacity aboard the *Monarch* (74) at the battle of Copenhagen on April 2nd 1801, the *Monarch* sustaining the highest casualties of any ship in the conflict, numbering 220, of which 57 were killed.

After serving in three further ships he joined the *Mars* (74) in April, 1803, where he attained the rank of Midshipman. Continuing in the *Mars*, he was present at the battle of Trafalgar, where he was slightly wounded in the leg.

His service continued in various ships, fighting in many actions and later becoming Sub-Lieutenant in March 1808. Following this he rose to Acting Lieutenant aboard the *Agamemnon* (64) in May 1810. Then, on the 4th February 1828, after much service aboard, he was appointed 1st Lieutenant aboard the *Blonde* (46) where he highly distinguished himself in unison with the French against Morea Castle, the last stronghold of the Turks in the Peleponnese islands. Commanding a breaching battery for twelve days and nights, his four guns expending 1.000 18lb shot and 6,000lbs weight of powder. For this service he was awarded the insignia of the Legion of Honour by the French, and the Redeemer of Greece by the Greeks. His promotion to Commander came in 1829, and after serving in several other ships, he was advanced to Captain in June 1838.

A brilliant career, beginning with the battle of Copenhagen at the age of nine.